NEW & SELECTED POEMS

NEW & SELECTED POEMS

BRIAN JONES

EDITED WITH AN INTRODUCTION BY

PAUL MCLOUGHLIN

Shoestring Press

All rights reserved. No part of this work covered by the copyright herein may be reproduced or used in any means – graphic, electronic, or mechanical, including copying, recording, taping, or information storage and retrieval systems – without written permission of the publisher.

Printed by imprintdigital
Upton Pyne, Exeter
www.imprintdigital.net

Typeset by types of light
typesoflight@gmail.com

Published by Shoestring Press
19 Devonshire Avenue, Beeston, Nottingham, NG9 1BS
(0115) 925 1827
www.shoestringpress.co.uk

First published 2013
Copyright © Brian Jones
Introduction copyright © Paul McLoughlin

The moral right of the author has been asserted

ISBN 978 1 907356 78 0

ABOUT THE AUTHOR

Brian Jones was born in 1938 in Islington and educated at Ealing Grammar School and Selwyn College, Cambridge, and worked mostly in adult education in Kent. He published several collections of poetry, first with Alan Ross's London Magazine Editions – *Poems* (1966); *A Family Album* (1968); *Interior* (1969); *Poems & A Family Album* (1972) and *For Mad Mary* (1974) – then with Michael Schmidt's Carcanet Press – *The Island Normal* (1980); *The Children of Separation* (1985) and *Freeborn John* (1990). *The Mantis Hand* (1970) is an Arc Publications pamphlet, and *The Spitfire on the Northern Line* (1975) is a collection for children published by Chatto & Windus in the Chatto Poets for the Young series. A further collection, *Burning Through The Fade*, remained unpublished at his death in 2009. *For Mad Mary* and *The Children of Separation* were PBS Recommendations. He was a recipient of a Cholmondeley Award in 1967 and a Gregory Award in 1968.

ACKNOWLEDGEMENTS

Shoestring Press is grateful to the editors of the following publications where the later poems or versions of them appeared: *London Magazine*, *Navis*, *PN Review*, and *Poetry Review*; to Noëlle Soret Jones for the poems published here for the first time; and to Michael Schmidt for permission to reproduce the introductory essay which first appeared in an earlier (and since much revised) version in *PN Review* 201 under the title 'Romantic Agoraphobia: The Poetry of Brian Jones'.

EDITOR'S NOTE ON SELECTION

Jones has a fondness for sequences and this led me to suppose it best not to excerpt from poems, that is to say to include or omit in full. I have excluded the title sequence from *For Mad Mary*, for example, because Mary is as wilfully independent as Miss Emily and may be represented by her. Emily, who is anyway the principal character of that poem, is already extensively represented elsewhere in this selection. And the poem is lengthy. I have deviated from this self-imposed rule on two occasions: first, in including only the 'Emily' section from *A Family Album* (all of its sections adopt the same verse form) and, second, in omitting some of the poems that make up the sequence 'Caesar's Progress'. I should not have so deviated had space allowed. 'At Varyinko' and 'Credits' in *For Mad Mary* and the first part of *The Island Normal* are taken to be sections rather than sequences and therefore available to be selected from. 'At the Zoo' (in *Interior*) is a group of three poems from which I have selected one. Poems previously published in magazines but not in book form carry an appropriate acknowledgement where they appear. Those previously unpublished anywhere are captioned as such.

Paul McLoughlin

CONTENTS

Introduction — xiii

from POEMS (1966)

Seeing My Wife Go Out Alone — 3
Husband to Wife: Party-Going — 4
Celebration—For Karen — 5
To a Wife Gone Away — 5
The Measure of the Need — 7
Miss Emily at Her Mother's Grave — 8
Visiting Miss Emily — 8
Two Preludes
   She Makes Pastry — 9
   He Drives — 9
A Garland for Edward Thomas — 11
Bed-Sit. Night — 12
Chrysanthemums — 13
Death of a Cat — 14
My Father — 15
How to Catch Tiddlers — 16
Stripping Walls — 17
The Garden of a London House — 18
Sunday Outing — 20
Thaw — 20

from A FAMILY ALBUM (1968)

Emily — 23

from INTERIOR (1969)

Smugglers' Route — 37
Trinket Box — 38
In a University Library — 39
A Girl's Words — 40
from At the Zoo: *Chi-Chi* — 42
Six Poems on Themes from Lorca — 43
A Wife's Tale — 47
Interior — 54

from FOR MAD MARY (1974)

from At Varykino:
    Gardening Sunday   57
    Chopping Wood   57
    Cathy, On Going to Turn out Her Light   58
    The Lane   59
    'At The Lane's End'   59
    4.10   60
from Credits:
    Stalled   60
    Cloud   61
    Relics for a Biography   62
The Courtenay Play   63

from THE SPITFIRE ON THE NORTHERN LINE (1975)

The Spitfire on the Northern Line   93
Bluebells   94

from THE ISLAND NORMAL (1980)

from 1. The Island Normal:
    Overnight   97
    The Island Normal   98
    Too Late   99
    End of Pier   99
    Return to Wasteground   100
    The Slaughterhouse Foreman's Son   101
    The Slaughterhouse Foreman's Daughter   101
    The Slaughterhouse Foreman's Wife   102
    A Slaughterer Watches   102
    Fearful   103
    March the Twenty-First   103
    In Memory: E.S.   104
    On the Edge   105
2. Aeneas And After:
    Horace Bids Farewell to Vergil   106
    Aeneas   108
    Aeneas Considers the Tribes   111
    On   112

Firstfoot	112
Firstfruit	113
Presence	113
To Sleep	114
A Release	114
The Dream	115
Upon Crappleton House	115

3. At Great Tew:

At Great Tew	119
Andrew Marvell Awaits His Charge	122

from THE CHILDREN OF SEPARATION (1985)

Introductory: 1944	127
Fancy Bread	130
At Badgers Mount	132
Approaching Islands	136
Talking	136
Snowmen	137
Earth Landing	137
A View	138
Oxford	138
The Children of Separation	139
Return Journey	140
No Small Murders	140

from FREEBORN JOHN (1990)

Introductory: 1638: Freeborn John	145
Stansted Sonnets (1–9)	146
from Caesar's Progress	
The Images of Caesar	151
Caesar's Progress	152
The Schooling of the Tribe	152
Caesar Chooses Leaders from the Tribe	154
Action Plan from Caesar's Inspectorate	155
Application for a Post in Caesar's Bureaucracy	156
Caesar's Circular, after Implementation of the Four Year Plan	159
For a Nativity	160
La Trahison d'un Clerc	161
Exiled Voices (1–9)	165

Letter from Elsewhere	174
Father and Son:	
My Father Begins to Tell his Story	176
My Father Reveals a Photograph	177
My Father's Last Meeting with his Father	179
My Father Sings in Church	179
My Father's First Job	180
My Father's Second Job	181
My Father Talks of his Life and Death	182
A View from the Boundary	184
Chess 1950	190
Q.E.D.	191
History 'O' Level	192
Headmaster	193
My River	194
Near Greenford, 1951	195
The Offer, The Refusal	196
After Tempest:	
Four Poems of Noëlle	197
Walk by Storm-Wrecked Wood	200
Autumn	201
Nature	201
At Stansted	202
Snowstorm Viewed From Love	203
I Think of Sisyphus	204

from BURNING THROUGH THE FADE
(uncollected & unpublished poems)

Manneville: The Museum of Resistance	207
Several Flauberts	208
29 Riverside Close Hanwell W7	209
Renoir's Girl	210
At Meopham Green	211
Different and Again	212
From the Album	213
Trails	213
Forerunner	214
Recognition	215
October	216

Chez	219
Oscar the Donkey	218
A Birth	219
Night of Separations	220
Day Out	220
From Voltaire's Garden and Other Entanglements	221

INTRODUCTION

THE POETRY OF BRIAN JONES
(born 10th December, 1938; died 25th June, 2009)

For the 10th Anniversary issue of *the Review* (Spring/Summer 1972), Ian Hamilton invited poets and critics to look back on the preceding ten years and comment on the state of poetry as they saw it. In his contribution to the resulting Poetry Symposium, John Carey cited Brian Jones as the most exciting new poet, beside Heaney, to have emerged during that period. By then, Jones had published three collections with Alan Ross's London Magazine Editions, the second of which, *A Family Album* (1968), had been one of Stephen Spender's Books of the Year. Reception had been for much the most part enthusiastic. *Poems* (1966) went into three impressions in six weeks, selling over a thousand copies and prompting interest from the national press—Jones was the subject of a news article in the pre-tabloid *Sun*, for example. A fourth and final collection with Alan Ross, *For Mad Mary* (1974), was followed by three with Carcanet between 1980 and 1990. Both *For Mad Mary* and *The Children of Separation* (1985) were Poetry Book Society recommendations.

And yet, in 1986, when Oxford University's John Sheeran, a fan of both football and poetry, compiled a 'British and Irish Poetry Rankings', set out in four divisions like the Football League of its day, Jones was nowhere to be found. Poets can lose their way, of course, but the attention Jones attracted early on (including a number of television appearances) invites us to question quite why he disappeared from view. It cannot be said that Jones was critically ignored, for his collections were widely reviewed, but he was not taken up by university English departments (nor did he teach in one). And although his work was occasionally included in anthologies, he rarely sent poems to magazines, the first collection of his requiring an acknowledgements page being *The Island Normal* (1980). When the publication of *The Children of Separation* (1985) was at a late planning stage, Jones asked for the poems to be returned to him because he had not retained anything like definitive copies of them. None of this is the stuff of marketing ambition. In an interview (published in *PN Review* 137, Jan–Feb 2001), he acknowledged that, after 'a period of silence', he realized that it was the writing itself that was important to him.

> It is not important in terms of being published, or being loved, or being recognised, but the actual process of writing, of working

at it, is absolutely vital for my life. It's a process I uniquely value, and I feel unhappy if I'm not engaged in it. All the rest is incidental.

How can a successful writer remain uninterested in publication? It is a position of selflessness that is more easily understood by those who knew the man, but there is reason to feel irritated by it, too. Brian Jones died in June 2009, leaving behind the manuscript of a 'new' book of poems written since his last collection, *Freeborn John* (1990). Some of the poems have appeared in *PN Review*, *London Magazine* and *Poetry Review*, but many have not. He spent the final decade of his life in Normandy with his second wife, Noëlle, and the happiness he found with her, and his discontent with the state of Thatcherite and post-Thatcherite England explain, at least in part, his apparent lack of desire to publish. The second section of 'From Voltaire's Garden and Other Entanglements' reads, in its entirety:

> When my neighbour (he lives a mile away)
> stopped at the gate to chat (so much to learn!)
> and asked whether I did not feel nostalgic
> for my homeland, I replied
> 'I do, yes, but no more than when I lived there.'
> (For a moment, I felt quite like my old self!)

It is this 'old self' who populates and informs Jones's early verse, and it is instructive to consider his journey in poetry from essential unease to the something more like poise he was to find later when feeling more at ease with himself. The final poems of his life were not free from pain, but by now the pain was that of political frustration, or of others, those voiceless or trapped or marginalized or resistant, like the Maquisards, and not the personal kind that had informed much of the early, highly-praised verse.

Some of the praise was unstinting. Gabriel Rosenstock thought that 'Seeing My Wife Go Out Alone' 'must be one of the finest poems of the decade.' It had 'a freshness, a moving intimacy, a delicately-balanced authority' that 'infused new life into English.' The poem's ending may remind us of the close of Larkin's 'Here' ('unfenced existence: / Facing the sun, untalkative, out of reach'), and remind us, too, of the fact that *The Whitsun Weddings* had appeared only two years before *Poems*, but Jones's final lines, however linguistically similar to Larkin, are none the less rooted in an existential terror that is closer in feeling to Plath than to the poet of 'Here'. The ending also does well to make us wary of the way in which the allure of literary biography is never far away in the study of Jones's work.

Another widely-praised and anthologized poem from Jones's first collection, 'Thaw' is a case in point, and a fine example of the way in which metaphor serves the lyric impulse to recreate. Read in the light of Jones's near-breakdown at Cambridge (he spoke in interview of 'night-sweats'), 'Thaw' takes on greater power and poignancy. Ideas of 'yearning' and 'susceptibility', of repressed desire, were central to Jones's early poetic, and while the poems were hailed as a fresh post-Movement approach to personal and domestic subjects, Jones said that the poems did not get near how he was really feeling at the time. Only 'Two Preludes' ('She Makes Pastry'; 'He Drives') gets close. This tension between revelation and reticence is important to an understanding of Jones's development.

He had gradually begun to look for ways of displacing the personal, but it took time. *A Family Album*, Jones's second collection, takes the form of four dramatic monologues, spoken by members of the same extended family, all of whom use the same original seven-line stanza with a single rhyme on 5 and 7. Here is Em as a wartime evacuee speaking of her Christian host in Bedfordshire, wanting to be with her younger sister, and how she'd 'moan' watching London trains go by:

> for the cats I'd had put down, for
> my Ada in Northampton,
> and for planes
> to drone this way, reducing her, Christ,
> cows, pigs to flames.

(The only other character in English poetry this brings to mind is Austin Clarke's differently realised and long-suffering Martha Blake.) Bill was Jones's father, Ada his mother, Fred his great-uncle, and Emily the real-life reclusive aunt he admired because she had endured and 'made pain home'. It is not difficult to see why he visited her during his troubled times. And these were their real names (given the slight change from Emma to Emily, which still facilitated 'Em'). But Jones calls himself David in perhaps a strained attempt to gain a measure of artistic distance. Whatever the reason, the book-length sequence remains powerfully unlike anything else in English poetry, and a pointer to the innovation that can arise from concentrated authenticity. Speaking of *A Family Album*, Jones said, 'I recognise that poetry and prose have different jobs to do, but I think that poets have unnecessarily lost too much ground to novelists in our time.'

It was with *Interior* (1969) that Jones began to find metaphors and personae that might serve to carry his personal concerns. Interestingly, in this collection, the speaker ceases to be suburban husband and father and becomes instead predominantly wife and mother. It was a volume much admired by Michael Longley, who believed that Jones was 'now delving deeper into the no man's land between his imagination and his circumstances':

> This involves three rewarding approaches. Firstly, he contemplates bravely his artistic ruthlessness and the darker areas of his own mind that are uncovered as a result. Secondly, he tries to isolate and so render archetypal and resonant the little ceremonies and rituals buried in the humdrum daily round and at the same time be true to the frightening biological simplicities they disguise, but also the merciful blurring they effect. Thirdly, he maps with a disquieting blend of fear and wonder feminine self-containment.

Interior also includes 'Six Poems on Themes from Lorca' in which we meet, among others, a young woman seeking fulfilment, and a woman embroidering. Lorca's Soledad Montoya becomes in Jones's sequence an unidentified woman in an indiscriminate location, whose agitated behaviour attracts alarm among villagers who ask where she goes and what she seeks, when all that lies beyond for them is 'ultimately, a bitter and restless sea / where to journey is to drown'. It is her agitation that Jones wishes to foreground. 'Already she moves among us, seeking / across huge plains of daylight, seeking', the woman's state of mind caught in the repetition of seeking as the end-word of successive lines. And the imagistic phrase 'huge plains of daylight', sandwiched by the repeated 'seeking', is characteristic of Jones's ability to surprise, 'daylight' serving almost as an abstraction, the grounded 'plains' failing to placate the infinity of all that exists beyond them, of all that is desired. In the fifth poem, the embroiderer (a nun in Lorca's original) looks to obsessive activity as a becalmer of wilder subterranean desires. Jones omits the more romantic, surreal images in a quest for a more concise lyrical directness. Clearly, he is unlikely to have followed so dramatic and romantic a lead as Lorca's. A poet who felt such a close affinity to Edward Thomas would have too much reserve. Jones strips his Lorcan sources of much of their imagery and symbolism and fashions a sequence of lyric poems in which he probes the tensions between repressed desire and social convention.

'The Courtenay Play', from *For Mad Mary*, charts the story of a self-styled knight who preached he was the Messiah and led, in Kent in 1838, an agricultural labourers' uprising that was ultimately crushed by military intervention. Much as it is difficult to think of forerunners in English verse for *A Family Album*, so, too, does one struggle to find precursors for this long poem set out as a play-within-a-poem in three Acts, with an 'Interval and Prelude'. Eventually the Courtenay figures were captured and, with sacks over their heads, shut in a barn, an image bound to resonate with Jones. The reasons for the uprising can easily be simplified (hardship, illiteracy, gullibility) but, rather than view the story as one of ignorant, vulnerable villagers succumbing to the impostured zeal of a megalomaniac, Jones looked to the psychological complexity of the motivations of Courtenay's followers. They were being offered something more than their daily round:

> When Courtenay came and on Boughton Hill
> sidled with the sun on a horse from Revelations
> and sent words bowling down the hill like stones,
> that night Curling dreamed.

Liardet the barrister commissioned to make a detailed report on the neighbourhood to the Central Society of Education, argues his case well, and it is to Jones's credit that he is allowed in the poem to do so. He claims to know what good is, which is 'freedom from wild and personal dreams'. Dreams 'must be contained. / The church contains them, and a well-run school.' Margaret Thatcher would have been proud of Liardet, whose own pride lies in the knowledge that his report helped to shape a school system for all. For Jones this meant not liberation but defeat. We become educated in order to silence ourselves. But the silence is civilized.

Prompted by his own experience, Jones became interested in the ways in which society treats insanity. He empathised with characters who could not or would not learn how to conform to the demands of those who would control them, characters who are marginalized in one way or another and prevented from offering the world what they have to offer it. Hence the epigraph to 'Exiled Voices', a quotation taken from the work of the clinical psychologist, David Smail: 'The greatest injustice done to people in our society is to rob them of a public life'. Smail's belief that the concept of therapy is largely ill-conceived also attracted Jones, who spent some time teaching creative writing in prisons and psychiatric units without ever for a moment regarding what he was doing as therapeutic. It was for him more real than that. It was a matter of facilitating voices.

Jones always admired acts of resistance. *Burning Through the Fade*, a collection that remained unpublished at his death, includes poems called 'Monuments des Maquisards' and 'Manneville: The Museum of Resistance'. And *Freeborn John* (1990) opens with 'Introductory 1638: Freeborn John', a poem that records how John Lilburne manages to circumvent all attempts to subdue him. Flogged 'from Fleet to pillory', his hands tied by his head, his mouth tamped with wadding, he amazes the witness still: 'O wonderful—I saw his feet / risk their small liberty to stamp ... stamp ... stamp.'

Jones may have found other, ostensibly more objective, vehicles for his central concerns but he continued to write personal and domestic poems. *For Mad Mary*, begins with a section called 'At Varykino' in which personal and domestic matters are seen through the refracting lens of Pasternak's Doctor Zhivago. *The Children of Separation* focuses with painful candour on the intimate details of relationships, including issues arising from the breakdown of a marriage. The title poem involves the volume's eponymous children, his own, while the impressive sequence, 'At Badger's Mount', deals with the personal fall-out. Jones is alert to the dangers of confusing life with art ('The images that others have of us / sustain and kill') and is careful not to claim the status of tragic hero:

> No end to the shame
> of the cultivated man once the sinking has begun
> and his sweating hand reaches to choose among
> Arnold, Milton, Shakespeare, Mogadon.

II

The Island Normal (1980), a collection that had shown Jones more aware of history as a poetic source, begins with a series of poems about the state of the then contemporary England, a group which, with other poems, bears scrutiny alongside poems about England and Englishness by Geoffrey Hill and Tony Harrison. The crumbling England that Brian Jones records in many of the poems in the title section is one of neglect and decay, but his view of the past and its people is complex. There are multiple Englands and he is alive to the dangers of nostalgia: his poems' speakers often know how feeling informs perception for good and ill. As in *A Family Album*, Jones's interest and his felt responsibility lie in a form of class-consciousness that compels him to speak for those who, as it were, cannot speak for themselves. In this sense, Jones is a political poet.

'At Great Tew', the first of two poems in the collection's third and final sequence to which it gives its name, is at once both a bleak, imagined narrative and a source of celebration. Jones is returning to Civil War England to help him understand its twentieth-century counterpart, and also to help him understand his own poetic. If Kropotkin, who provides the epigraph for the collection's first section, advocated mutual aid, a world based on co-operation rather than conflict, what draws Jones to Carey, Viscount Falkland, is the despair that led him to commit suicide in a reckless act of bravery born of his realisation that the Civil War was not about to reach any speedy, or even-handed, conclusion. Falkland had opposed the policies of Charles I, but later became the king's secretary of state when the puritans assumed power and were clearly uninterested in compromise.

Jones's narrative finds Falkland in low spirits: 'As he could not heal his country's disease, / he longed for death.' He is, like Aeneas, a leader of men. In the early morning light: 'Across an English field he stares / into the mirror of an English field / where small fires blossom. / Between the fields, the dark fume of a hedge, / and a linking gap'. The 'linking gap' should be an opportunity for compromise, but it remains implacably a way through to meet the enemy in battle. Falkland bemoans 'the simplicity of alignment', people's seemingly endless desire to belong at whatever cost, a simplicity that leads 'inexorably / to a misty field at dawn'. When battle commences, he heads for 'that gap / clean in the hedge where image coincides / with image and a hail of lead'. It is the manner of his death that brings the two sides together, if only fleetingly, in a passage that reminds of Marvell's 'Horatian Ode': 'Comrades / and foes, stunned, rein back to admire / this career of death momently'. But it is the admiration of incomprehension.

The kind of world Falkland despaired of is suddenly brought up to date, as if we had been reading about it all whilst picnicking: 'The Sunday paper brightly features / 'suicide chic', the hagiography / of exemplary failures'. 'Suicide chic' would have horrified Kropotkin, but a world of sound bites and immediacy does not care to probe reasons. Jones's poem memorably concludes:

> The Sunday's camera would have caught it well:
> that split astonished second when
> two hell-bent forces faltered as there lay
> between them a small island of one man;
> until one side saw in the death
> bravery flowering from a certain cause,
> the other, panic from a loss of nerve,
>
> and craning forward, screaming, both came on.

The 'small island of one man' takes us back to the crumbling England with which *The Island Normal* began, and in doing so illustrates why Jones thinks of the entire collection as one poem. The opposing views of 'bravery' and 'loss of nerve' illustrate the provisionality that remains one of his quintessential concerns. For all this, however, *The Island Normal* also includes personal reflections, including an elegy to Aunt Emily that ends: 'Thank you for everything. / Old atheist-hypochondriac-anarchist, who knew / the world was crazy, embodied it, and laughed'.

III

Much of Jones's verse concerns those on the edges of things, those who have been (or choose to be) marginalized, those living on faultlines, such as people who live at thresholds; they exist in the liminal state of being neither-this-nor-that, of belonging and not-belonging, and they resist, consciously or otherwise, the processes of normalisation. 'Fearful' illustrates this tension by contrasting a romantic yearning for travel and experience with an agoraphobia that holds him back. Jones's family moved from Islington to a post-war prefabricated house in Greenford, where he was the only grammar school boy on the estate. His growing educational estrangement from his local peers and from his own parents led to the kind of neither-this-nor-that state of being that is exemplified by the romantic-agoraphobic dichotomy and produced what for Jones became an abiding and telling image: 'When I was a child and real I lay / on our tar roof and itched for the world.'

The opening poem in the 'Aeneas and After' sequence pits home-loving Horace against a Vergil driven to travel. The book's title-poem, 'The Island Normal', deals with leaving and returning to an England that is both home (a concept of importance in its different ways to both Horace and Aeneas, and, as it were, to both faces of Jones) and a repository of frustration and limitation. This is another poem in which Jones speaks as 'we', for both himself and his wife, and by implication for all others who feel similarly: 'So often we push off from it, bored stiff / by its rightness, taking ages to jettison / the blue prescription of its near-shore waters'.

Returning, getting back, however, is 'miraculous, it's really miraculous'. The Island heaves up 'as if unanchored and full of compassion', precisely those attributes it seems devoid of when familiar. Suddenly the bay's blues are 'gorgeous' and 'stepping on to the jetty, the wood creaking, / we're primed, it feels, like Odysseus with marvels'. Even this euphoria is qualified, however: 'But since we've been nowhere, precisely Nowhere, / of all those quiet Normalists, who shore-based know / the obvious horrors of ocean, who will listen?' Interestingly, Jones grants both 'Nowhere' and 'Normalists' the capitals of allegory, as if they were a real place and its inhabitants, because learning about normality and learning to normalise ourselves gains us access to everywhere civilised and thus to the accommodating boredom that is nowhere. Not wishing to stay but feeling uncomfortable elsewhere dooms the individual to the fearful in-between state of the romantic agoraphobic.

The very idea of England is problematical in a post-colonial age. Tony Harrison's Leeds is both England-as-region and region-as-Britain (if not world). Other nations can fly their flags with impunity and pride. England's is too much associated with football hooliganism, and is anyway not British. It is in this new dispensation OK to say you are Scots or Welsh or Northern Irish, but not that you are English. Brian Jones confronted this difficulty some while back: 'My passport said 'British'. / I resented that. / The boots slamming on continents.' There will be those crass enough to find this xenophobic, but it wants to confront its real identity, not one foisted on it (*pace* The Act of Union). Geoffrey Hill would approve:

> Keep what in repair?
> Or place what further
> toll on the cyclic
> agony of empire?
> ('To The High Court of Parliament', *Canaan*)

Jones had no Welsh connections. Nor was he a religious man. All this is important because he shared much of the unease, even despair, and the almost desperately self-willed hope of Hill and Harrison, without the religious angst of Hill or the regional class-consciousness of Harrison (though class is also close to Jones's heart). Part of the problem of Jones's reception is that he came from London. Better to come from or represent one of the regions. Islington is not Bromsgrove, nor is it Leeds. It is therefore suspect, though the most cursory glance at the work will show a poet anxious to follow in the footsteps of the Blake he greatly admired, the Blake who believed, as Eliot has observed that 'the ordinary processes of society which constitute education for the ordinary man . . . consist largely in the acquisition of impersonal ideas which obscure what we really are and feel, what we really want, and what really excites our interest'.

Jones is also, as Michael Cayley has observed, a poet of feeling rather than ideas. He was pained by Thatcherite Britain. Hence 'A View from Stansted', a village in Kent that is not the airport, where 'A cold vision is settling into place: barbed / certainties that mark red in the balance-sheet / the questioner, the immigrant, the reflective; / it crushes discourse beneath its monologue / and proves dreams pathology'. Ten years earlier, in *The Island Normal*, Jones had surveyed an England of crumbling props. 'End of Pier', which might as well be 'End of England', concludes: 'A small 'if only' / has gone, a yearning, a huddled / discreet town's V sign at itself'. Jones, like Hill, engages nostalgia without idealizing it. This is a seaside resort (and a poetry) fully alert to its own ironies. Jones is writing post-Romantic poetry that is endeavouring to be pre-Romantic.

What he searches for is the kind of poise he finds in Andrew Marvell, who managed to balance all manner of political, artistic and personal imperatives to satisfying effect. The excellent poem, 'Andrew Marvell Awaits his Charge' (in 1653, Marvell became tutor to Oliver Cromwell's ward) repays the closest attention and outlines a kind of manifesto:

> It is my duty to maintain
>
> A tightrope discipline of mind
> My present to the future which
> Approaches, nervous as a hind,
> Green fields, or slaughter in a ditch.

This is not only Marvell speaking, but Jones, too. Hill may temperamentally prefer Donne, Herbert, Vaughan and Crashaw, but he does still ask (in the third of *Canaan*'s three poems called 'To the High Court of Parliament'): '—who could outbalance poised / Marvell'.

This search for poise, however, did not preclude Jones from showing his anger at the way things are. He spent a career in adult education. His despair is with the self-congratulatory mindlessness that supposes it cares in some impressively modern way, with management-speak about 'the way forward' and being 'robust'. And if you demur you are sent to an outpost. In *Freeborn John*, the sequence 'Caesar's Progress' hilariously satirizes this Orwellian march of mediocrity. The excesses of all earlier ages have been tamed: 'Nothing radical has happened. / And in any case it is now all over.' The sequence carries an epigraph from arguably Hill's finest extended poem, *The Mystery of the Charity of Charles Peguy*: 'This is your enemies' country which they took / in the small hours an age before you woke'. It seems Jones's Aeneas was prescient in asking at Carthage when he wakes worrying about readiness and provisions: 'Are / these the new gods—Detail? Banality?'

The poise and peace of mind hinted at in the poems that bring both the 1985 and 1990 volumes to a close—poems of praise and gratitude, and no little surprise, arising from a new and settled relationship—are temporarily interrupted by Jones's abhorrence of Thatcher's Britain. He found in the 1987 hurricane and a village in Kent a rich poetic source for the dramatization of kinship and anomie. *Freeborn John* brings out the political poet in Jones more directly than any earlier collection. Peter Bland regarded it as Jones's best, the culmination of 'a continuous thirty year commentary from the backroom of the dispossessed'. William Scammell, described it as 'honourably bewildered by what there is left to believe in' and it is this bewilderment that distinguishes Jones from the Muldoons of the world. He can be humorous with the best of them but he is not playful (though he enjoyed this very quality in Foucault). Nor is he as relentlessly or religiously troubled as Geoffrey Hill (even in witty mode), finding no need to wrestle with a God he did not believe in. Nor was he trying, like Lowell and Plath, to bully language into submission. From where he stood, what else was there save a bewilderment that knows it belongs to what it is bewildered by?

Paul McLoughlin

FURTHER READING

Michael Cayley, 'Where Walls Take Root: Some Thoughts on the Poetry of Brian Jones', *Poetry Nation* No. 2, 1975

John Killick,'The Ache of Wholeness: An Introduction to the Poetry of Brian Jones', *The North* 15, 1994

Peter Bland, 'Messages from the Edge: A Second Look at the Poetry of Brian Jones', *Poetry Review* (Vol.89 No.2, Summer 1999)

Brian Jones in Conversation with Paul McLoughlin, *PN Review* 137 (Vol.27 No.3, January–February 2001)

Paul McLoughlin, 'Romantic Agoraphobia', *PN Review* 201 (Vol.38. No.1, September–October 2011)

from POEMS (1966)

SEEING MY WIFE GO OUT ALONE

Left at the window, helpless at your going,
Watching unusual space lengthen between us,
I note a jaunty step I once desired,
Hips heaving, head still lacking confidence,
Arms rather stiff, the shoulders tensioned high—
Bizarre regalia of a puzzling mind
That won me to you seven years ago.
I see now I have failed to liberate,
That liberation is not part of love.
I've watched your shoulders sag with tenderness
Over the hunger of our suckling child;
Nothing I've felt so soft as your bare arms
Across my back at midnight or at dawn;
Your head lolls back in laughter frequently
On neck pliant and nerveless. And yet now,
As distance interposes, you resume
Your solitary history, and I know
It is not distance only—loss of me,
My touch, our child—occasions this old style.
I've learnt more intimately this is defeat,
Lying on your soft belly, joined
Still at the thighs, and at the breast by sweat,
Not daring to raise my face from your pillowed hair
To find your eyes wide open, scanning
Unchallenged space, where all the questions start.

HUSBAND TO WIFE: PARTY-GOING

Turn where the stairs bend
In this other house; statued in other light,
Allow the host to ease you from your coat.
Stand where the stairs bend,
A formal distance from me, then descend
With delicacy conscious but not false
And take my arm, as if I were someone else.

Tonight, in a strange room
We will be strangers: let our eyes be blind
To all our customary stances—
Remark how well I'm groomed,
I will explore your subtly-voiced nuances
Where delicacy is conscious but not false,
And take your hand, as if you were someone else.

Home forgotten, rediscover
Among chirruping of voices, chink of glass,
Those simple needs that turned us into lovers,
How solitary was the wilderness
Until we met, took leave of hosts and guests,
And with delicate consciousness of what was false
Walked off together, as if there were no one else.

CELEBRATION—FOR KAREN

Outside, ice begins
and a moon locked among frost-prickings
of stars is taut with light.
Silence hardens round our city. What
can move, what can disturb? Traffic
will not intrude tonight; the docks
are tranced with cranes, and ships
nudge the oiled wharves as if in sleep.

We shall not trade again on seas we crossed
and haunted when the times were hard,
when times were loss and barter and exchange
of the most personal for the new and strange.
Now we sit where firelight unifies
us and the room—constructed certainties.

TO A WIFE GONE AWAY

A starved and skulking spring. A few primroses
coldly daub the banks. The sensitive
might hear the groans of trees
leaning upon locked buds. I hear nothing,
write nothing. The paper is coy and chaste
under my need. And you are silent. The only growth
is lust. Lust smears my flesh, maddens. I have become
a scorch and sprout between the legs
because you are absent, silent. Passing hags
strut with sensual virtues, schoolgirls
triumph across my view, and now
I would not know you from them. You have no history.
I have scorched your voice away, your tenderness.
You are a fragment, one of the bellies, groins
I slink among. O climb out of my head,
that tight silence! Remind me. Be gathered
and complete again. The hot need
goads and crazes, but what's lost of you
torments with a long ache to be recalled.

THE MEASURE OF THE NEED

The storm keeps us awake. The wind
bruises the house, smacks open the yard door,
savages it. Against my thigh
your knuckles harden, reminding me not to sleep.

I am remembering what you said
was it an hour ago? was it about
some fear of thunderous nights? I can recall
no words, but total fright

and a wind battering. We are far
out in the dark, and what are words,
if I murmur them, but curtains in a draught,
usurped and menacing. To lie apart

in a threatened home, to buffet
down vast nights, while every small
habit of self and daylight bobs
away on darkness, is no nightmare, love,

being the measure of the need that makes
dearer the way the dawn gathers your face,
settles curtains, and reinstates
my presence through the awareness in your hand.

MISS EMILY AT HER MOTHER'S GRAVE

On my knee-joints, stones;
earth-crumbs among roots thrusting
into my handbones—these
have been since I first came,
since they fixed you here, made
you a place for me to visit.
If I look up
carefully, the air not disturbed,
nothing moves. We are alone.
We are as we were.
You will understand I have no flowers.
They say 'Go quietly to her room
if you must go. If she sleeps
do not tamper with her pillow.'
Here I am, to press bone against stone.
I would not adjust your permanence with flowers.

VISITING MISS EMILY

When you visit Aunt Em you must whistle
Through railings, and her face will glide
Like a slow white moon to the window-space.

Then you must wait patiently
By the bruised door—(put your ear
Against it, you will hear how slow she comes).

When it opens, say with unusual breeziness
How are you then? but don't listen
For an answer. Instead, go down

Stairs murky as a lost century
And emerge in her underground cavern
Where a cat will panic in the darkness.

There, make as much noise as you can—

Hum, whistle, scrape a chair—before
She enters with that curious and catching malady

Of never having been or done anything.
While you stay, be on your guard.
She is a siren, although she weighs five stone

From some illness she has never recovered from.
Although her hair is thin and lank as a washing-up rag,
Although she keeps a finger crooked to stop a ring falling off.

Soon she will be capering for you, telling stories
Of how during the war she'd dive under the bed
So that the falling bomb would bounce back from the springs;

Of how the sole stripped from her shoe, and she walked
A mile sliding her foot to stop the cod's-mouth flap—
She flickers to life with visits; she forgets,

And soon you'll be groaning and wheezing, helpless.
But keep your wits about you; remember she
Is your kin. Haven't you seen somewhere

That paleness of eyes? that pallor of cheeks?
Haven't you known what it is to slump like that?
Isn't this cavern familiar? and the filtered daylight?

Wish her goodbye. Kiss her cheek as if it were lovely.
Thank her for the soft biscuits and the rancid butter.
Then straighten your tie, pull your cuffs square,

Think of tomorrow as a day when the real begins
With its time and teabreaks. Tell her you'll
Visit her again sometime, one quiet Sunday.

TWO PRELUDES

I. *She Makes Pastry*

My old voluptuary, spreading coolly
under my fingers, swooning at my touch,
fat-blobs smirch your features.
You are flat under me, puffy and compliant.
I curve my nail thus and you smile,
thus and you cry.
I hate you how you are good to me.
Do my tears scald? Feel how they scald
your lax and sallow cheeks—your loony face
smiles weak with love!
Feel this curved nail stab down—
you reward my palps with cool pleasure!
I crush you—and your soft love slinks
foolish and faithful out through my hands
to gaze at me. I hate you how you wait,
boneless, in smile, for my skill on you
to fashion the usual success. See, I pound
your oblivion, pummel your mute
insidious love, and still you cling
and clutch at fingers, and your dust
welcomes the dark lapse of my tears.

My hands stray—look, they brush at daylight,
do other things. O God maintain
the precarious, teetering skill of my hands!

II. *He Drives*

Come soon, creature—
Rabbit, maimed bird, hare,
—Scut from these straggling trees
So that the foot will plunge,

The car lose confidence, whimper, squeal, swerve,
The trees rise up and wait,
And the waked sense chatter along the blood
To redefine me.

Creature, in shadow
Somewhere you prolong
Cruelly this torment of watching
Two hands, sallow and deft, move
Like another's hands an indifferent yard away,
Of being lips to a cigarette,
A swollen tongue to smoke, the eyes with which
A mirror watches—

Bits of a broken
Purpose, a litter
Of meaning scattered functioning into void.
I drive fast for you, creature.
My hope is rigid in the flesh, my head dollish,
A mask in smile. I hear lamps
Beat past, endurance mortal in their time. Your trees
Give out.

I have no message
For hands to sweat by,
No prayer for your sharp scuttle across my brain.
I only see high concrete arms
Swoop and swoop with dangling unlit lamps
And over roofs a white spire stride,
Hunting roadwards, its menace stiff and chill
With unconcern.

A GARLAND FOR EDWARD THOMAS

I

There will always be woods, and from their brink
A road catching the sun, prompting journey
And promising arrival. There will always be
Someone to travel it—to reach at night
The first village, drink the local beer,
Question the suspicious, receive no answer,
Book a room, get a goodnight from some,
Then lean across the sill and watch the road
Making for somewhere else under the moon,
Prompting a journey, promising arrival.

II

The sky tilts westward. The sun is massy and sinks
While the moon on the eastern upswing cloudily floats.
From the fields and the scarred hills a fume of darkness seeps.
A wood slowly extends itself. Houses fuse
Then trickle darkly outwards—the intimate land
You knew well, where in lanes brimming with light
The slightest flowers were your familiars, where scabs of shade
Peeled off with the wind, and the sun snoozed in mild brick
Or buttressed the bulk of trees and made the hills gentle.
But now the thickets flower with chaos, the
Owl gloats and the unvibrant moon takes charge
And what can the walker do but think of others
Intensely, the lonely and poor, the humanisers,
And clutch hope that a world spilling over its line
Is on the far side of his eyes, and the night's doing?

III

An image persists. It is of you
Hand-cradling a wren's egg, sensing all
The perilous warm promise of the shell.

IV

When the trench blurred, when the parapet
Crumpled and swam, when the frail
Lines sketched by your forty years
Dissolved once more and finally, could you know
What was perishing, what charity, what
Intricate design of love and wants?
Never to have found self—it is this that haunts,
And your searching, and your awkwardness of voice.
There fell
An eye that scanned dark, and distinguished plants,
An honesty that shirked a specious noise.

BED-SIT. NIGHT

Shirts hang from rails
(I finger a slack sleeve straight)
Shoes are aligned
An empty jacket waits

And back through fingers
At ebb upward through arm
Employment's fury dwindles
Into alarm

While space hardens
Against line of shirt and shoe.
A last tamper of fingers
And what choice has brought me to

Is rigid and voiceless
Shrunk beyond will and stir
Where a jacket hangs stiff
With tomorrow's character.

CHRYSANTHEMUMS

They are poised and exuberant in a shop prim with clippers
and grey powders that quell whatever teems and breeds
and a man that handles stems with fingers like disinfectant.
They blazon 'This is our season. We are a fulfilment of a time,
a gold embodiment', and the great clumps of their heads among
the soft greens of flimsier flowers, and lolling tongues
of lap-dog pot-plants, smoulder their being, their contained fury.
I carry them in a cowl of tissue and punctuate walls with them.
They are engrossed with all the myths of autumn; they issue burning
immediate from bud, cram their short space with fire,
proclaiming 'Now Now Now'. They compel you to be wise.
They force life to the nerve-ends of their petals; they shrivel
with the fact but not the fear of death; they are obsessed
with the instant, not with summer buried by horizons—I could learn
from these guests, I tell myself, lying. If I could
revel in lucky wisdoms, and when they flop and shrivel
sweep the debris away like these spent shreds, I could enter
the brain-house in cold season, never to meet
Regret, hunched, fondling unexploited scraps.

DEATH OF A CAT

Always fastidious, it removed its dying
From us, and lay down by it in the dark
As if death were a mouse, and a cat's rôle
To deal with it, and not involve the house;
Chose a remote spot that, when I bent to help,
Shocked because it existed—I had thought
The mind a complete map of home; left dust
On my fingers when I had settled it
In front of the fire on an old blanket;
Insisted to the last on standing
And walking with frail dignity to its water
In its usual place in the kitchen, disdaining
The saucer we had thoughtfully set near it.

And death was a wind that tested regularly
The strength the cat had left, and in its walk
Puffed on its flank and made it totter
Then courteously desisted. Death can wait.
Powerless, with crude tears, we watched the cat
Totter and reassert itself again and again
Its life the fuel for its will to live
Until the bones appeared, blood dried in veins,
The pelt was ragbag remnants, the eyes gone out
And the wind's task was easy and the cat fell.

MY FATHER

    I

rose like a warrior
each day at six, set hearth ablaze
in a trice, with bacon salted the air,
and gorged. It was his hour

and dark preserved it. At seven
the station claimed him. I'd hear
a brisk exit, sometimes whistling.
My job was opening curtains.

    II

He is dead. You'll find his eyes
in mine, his shape of hands
contoured in my skin. His best
gift he did not leave—how

to be alone an hour
and use it well, then stride
out into frowsy light, the day
surrendered, but not counted lost.

HOW TO CATCH TIDDLERS (for Stephen)

Watch the net drift. Grey tides
Mingle what purposes your eye supposed
But watch the net. There is no fish
Only the net, the way it moves. There is no fish,
Forget the fish. The net is spread
And moving. Steer gently. Keep the hand
Pressured constantly against the stream.
There is no catch now, only the net
And your pressure and your poise. Below,
Ignore the pebbles and the promising weed
Mooning over its secrets. There is just the net,
The hand, and, now, near an old glance somewhere,
A sleek shape holding its body constant,
Firm in its fluid world. Move on. Watch
Only the net. You are a hand only,
Steering, controlling. Now look.
Inside that silent bulge the shape
Breaks black and firm. You may rise,
You may rise now—the deftest
Turn of wrist will do it. Your hand
Crude again can support the cling of mesh.
You can relax, coldly note
The titchy black squirm. You have achieved.
Commit success to jamjars. Lean again.
Dip the slack net. Let it belly.

STRIPPING WALLS

I have been practical as paint today, wholesome as bread—
I have stripped walls. I rose early and felt clean-limbed
And steady-eyed and said 'Today I will strip those walls.'
I have not been chewing my nails and gazing through windows
And grovelling for the subject or happiness. There was the subject,
Simple and tall. And when the baker called he was civil
And looking at me with some respect he said
'I see you're stripping walls'—I could see he liked me.
And when I opened the door to the greengrocer, I glinted my eyes
And leaned nonchalantly and poked some tomatoes and said as an aside
'I'm stripping walls today.' 'Are you?' he asked, interested, and I said
'Yes, just stripping those walls.' I could feel my forearms thicken, grow
Hairy, and when the laundry arrived I met it with rolled sleeves.
'Stripping walls?' he asked. 'Yeah,' I said, as if it were unimportant,
'Stripping walls. You know.' He nodded and smiled as if he knew.
And with a step like a spring before the meal I strode
Down to the pub and leaned and sipped ale and heard them talk
How one had cleared land that morning, another chopped wood.
When an eye caught mine I winked and flipped my head. 'I've been
Stripping walls,' I said. 'Have you?' 'Yeah, you know, just stripping.'
They nodded. 'Can be tricky,' one mumbled. I nodded. 'It can be that.'
'Plaster,' another said. 'Holes,' I said. 'Workmanship,' said another
And shook his head. 'Yeah, have a drink,' I said.
And I whistled through the afternoon, and stood once or twice
At the door-jamb, the stripper dangling from my fingers.
'Stripping?' asked passing neighbours. I nodded and they went on happy—
They were happy that I was stripping walls. It meant a lot.

When it grew dark, I went out for the freshness. 'Hey!' I called up,
'I've been stripping walls!' 'Just fancy that!' answered the moon with
A long pale face like Hopkins. 'Hey, fellers!' he called to the stars,
'This hairy little runt has been stripping walls!' 'Bully for him,' chimed
The Pole star, remote and cool as Vergil, 'He's a good, good lad.'
I crept to the kitchen, pursued by celestial laughter.
'You've done well today,' she said. 'Shall we paint tomorrow?'
'Ah, shut up!' I said, and started hacking my nails.

THE GARDEN OF A LONDON HOUSE

The garden of a London house;
New tenants yearly—
It wasn't hard to find excuse
For looking rarely

At coarsening grass and riotous hedge
And earth trod solid,
Easier still never to budge
And work upon it.

But something in the April airs
This Sunday morning
Prevailed. I borrowed fork and shears
And fell to working

Shy in my shirtsleeves. Blunted steel
Yanked grass like tweezers
And taught me the more patient skill
Of snipping pieces

Deft from the blade-tops, in a slow
Whittling down
Towards the packed root-stalks, all yellow,
Dank from no sun.

And here, in this low world, my gaze
(First time for months)
Focused; things from void took size;
I witnessed ants

Spontaneously appear on stones,
A magic spider,

A snail's intense life through its horns'
Translucent quiver.

To shape the hedge from its neglect
I used a saw,
Relished each merciless attack,
Each soft white scar,

And how the clipped leaves from the shears
Leapt and swarmed down,
And how on the grey street appeared
Unusual green.

And now, washed, tired, in starched, clean shirt,
With blistered hands,
I gaze where I have made a start
To make amends,

And taste a weariness again
That is a pleasure
And marvel as a windless rain
Unlocks such savour

As I remember once to have known,
Or perhaps never,
For I have been long in a town
And am not a gardener.

SUNDAY OUTING

So the dog still yelps at the door
We slammed within an inch of his snout,
And the washing jerks unharvested,
Spoiling in the rain-laced wind
Five miles away in our backyard,
And the hag from below can make her stealthy climb,
Enter and pilfer as usual the rooms we forget to lock,
And perhaps the tap is running, the sink blocked,
Gas escaping, kitchen filling. Forget it. Watch
Through the windscreen (tick-tocked clear) the downs
Darkening with the rainy mist; let your flesh
Relax into the damp freedom (chuck that fag away);
Tell me (look this way damn you) tell me do you feel
An old design return? Do you recall hour after hour
Spent watching dusk or dawn inch up? What was your head
Vacant with then? Tell me, love, what did I speak of?
How did we manage without dogs and hags?

THAW

Suddenly air is careless, generous,
caressing where it gripped. On lawns
the snowmen shrink to tiny pyramids
their eyes of frizzled coke roll out like tears
the blackbird launches song on running streams
and rising like a tide the grass
wells over snow and leaves it islanded
while hills like withheld waves tremble to move.

Time lives again. There are ripples, rivulets
in lanes and gutters, shimmers across bark;
stones and jutting tree-roots shine, while
the heart that through the rigid months became
a memory of spring, an easy yearning,
must be itself again, trembling, susceptible.

from A FAMILY ALBUM (1968)

EMILY

i

Eldest. Little old woman
from the start. Loved horses
clacking nodding over cobbles.
Punched once by a carter who flogged
shivering flanks till I bled tears
ran shouting up to him
ended up on my arse.

Liked the way cats padded
for food, padded off, kept neat,
were ill in corners.
Mother worked. I fed kids,
kissed, soaped them, shoved
all into bed. And it
was horses and cats I loved.

Ada, though, she was
a beauty, lovely little kid.
When she was born her nails
so faintly there, took my breath away.
And that milky smell. She turned,
when I held her, to my tits.
My face burned.

London was my world—the part
where they piggy-backed kids to school
for lack of shoes, where gas-lamps
swelled and shrank the street,
draped it with shadows,
where grotesques sat on corners, took bets,
grinned from windows.

Mornings were dirty. I traipsed
for years to the jew's place,
bent in a line of benders over cloth,
stitched gaudy clothes, listened
to unseen horses' hooves
cracking the cobbles, dared not speak,
slyly watched clouds and roofs.

Grew skinny with bad ears, cared
for beauty only in my Ada,
on Fridays curled her hair for her, shaped
frocks for her from remnants of the jew's.
She was lovely, leisured,
haughty, undaunted by school,
she was family-treasured,

like the Klondyke nugget, brought
by Uncle Fred, or the model ship
our father carved, when a Pacific calm
fastened him in blue—
so remote and rare was she,
fragile and small, a frail
shaving of a possibility.

ii

Hastings: a three-day charity trip—
shocked by the sea and sleeping alone—
a metal comb scraping my scalp for fleas—
hands soaping me, probing clothes for lice
and me for sores—
me ashamed of my scraggy arms
and the holes in my drawers.

The first morning, shrunk by the wind,
I stood on the sea-front, watching small
tough men handle rods, and send
a weighted line hissing miles in a quick curve—
another breed
from me and my Londoners, squat, firm-faced,
I felt a weed

as their kids in the shocking wind
rasped twine through their fingers, managed hooks,
while their wives sat on stones, knee-hunched,
unflinching, in a trance of competence.
Then I saw
a landed fish flip separate from shingle
its gills red-raw

and kick up suddenly, writhe and squirm,
and flop hopeless back on stones. And there
and there and there and all over were fish
fish fish fish gaping, twitching, eyes aghast,
dying and dead
and women sat among them, watching
or chewing bread.

On a bench, away from wind, in a
small tattered garden for the old,
among old men with dripping noses, and old
women crooning alone, or talking death,
I sat moaning and white
crying for London. When I undressed they beat me,
seeing my new drawers stained with shite.

iii

Ada found Bill one day
outside her work, bent tying up a shoe
already knotted—told her
he'd loved her months
in secret—just what not to do
with a bitch like Ada—
soon learnt it, too,

and got hell, from that flounce
of bubbly curls, from that quick sneer
that taunted his stiffness, taunted
how he rarely laughed. I told her straight
she took the piss
too often—warned her straight.
But one kiss

and a blue look from those eyes, and he
was grovelling and grateful. But,
Christ, he had a temper. You'd see
him snap behind his eyes,
his lips pale,
and they'd be at it, wrecking my bloody room,
with me, frail

as a tit in a thunderstorm, hid
by the one unliftable chair. Jars,
cups, forks, plates smacked walls,
doors, each other. Language!
you never heard
such language—vile, it was vile. Then
I'd hear their words

move towards sex, abusive still, but
sex-vile. It was wooing, it was
how they met in the wreckage, striking,
but in lust now, and they'd fall,
gripping on my bed.
It was then I'd get out, buy cat's fish, or
whatever entered my head.

But I liked Bill, liked him a lot,
liked what Ada called his stiffness
and I called pride, a kind
of dignity. Seeing him come
down our scruffy street
with flowers in his fist,
his feet

awkward and shy—the kind
that kids stopped playing to look at, wondering
whether to jeer and follow,
not one of them, not quite—
his body stiff
as he passed them—a man
walking a cliff,

tense against the fall. And then
we found out why, why he was awkward, why
touchy as a nettle. It took
three months before
she saw his home
and then it was a note that said
Bill wants you to come.

And what she found left her crying half the night
with me dangling beside her, helpless, mute,
listening to it all. He lived
in Raer Street, a real slum,
in a basement and first floor
with his parents and eight others,
the door

wedged open, never shutting. When
she went in the dark and stench
it made her sick. He lay
in a room stained brown against the bugs, a mac
chucked over him,
gasping for breath with asthma,
and crying,

crying like a woman, wheezing out
'You shouldn't've come. I never asked.
I never asked at all' and biting
his fist with shame and rage. And when
she came out weeping
she found his father bronchial in a chair
twisted and sleeping

and the old girl washing cups
in a scummed bath, wiping up
on a shirt-tail. Well,
that was that. Ada was caught.
When he got well
they got engaged. It didn't stop
them giving hell

to each other still, but she understood
and loved the stiffness of him, and he
grew confident because of it, began
to boss even me about,
a bit of a know-all,
full of advice I didn't want to hear
when I fell ill.

Suddenly said one day (and she
was by the door and ready with my coat)
'Bugger the cats' ears. *You* got ears
and a mess they are.
Come on.
We're going to the Royal Free
to get them done.'

My God the fright—just thinking of it now
I want to pee. There I was,
him nearly holding me down on the trolleybus,
groaning and pleading with them 'Bill,
tomorrow, Bill. I promise.'
And Ada half-enjoying it, the bitch—
Christ, she likes others

stupid, or grovelling for her.
Then there I sat, among old spewing men,
with the stink of ether sickening me,
and nurses thumping past with silver trays
glinting with knives—
That was enough for me. He let go once. I'd
gone past waddling wives,

past shuffling bedrobed skeletons,
belting like Old Mother Riley, legs
akimbo, slipping, slithering on the shine,
shins cracking corners, through a door,
out into air.
By the time they'd found the exit, looked around,
I wasn't there,

was sitting in a trolley in a faint,
heading for Barnet, for the terminus.
Daft. I was daft. I know it now.
And as soon as autumn fogs come down
I pay for it. And when
winter shuts me up with my weaknesses
I doubly wish that time again.

iv

John. Your memory handles me
in remoter nights. You would still
know that bridge. I know it still.
Its walls seep. The canal stinks.
Kids scrawl on putrid brick
with chalk or stone
and bits of stick

J loves E I want to screw
you Jane. The bank is perilous with slime.
The day you reported dead
I went there, slipped
and screamed into the mud
lusts lusts
fancied it your blood.

They washed me like a child,
put me to bed. Some fretful nights
an old maid remembers
you and timidities.
That last time O your hands
were brash. Under them
I seeped and stank

ashamed, was open and wanted
and wanted. Felt you throb hard
rise dig my leg. Lay on slime
was slime was open
and wanted and wanted.
But where lamps
and moon slanted

under the bridge swam suddenly with tears.
The choke of your mouth, your
vast tongue choking me, the squirm
of your belly were brutes. I battered them off.
I still smooth my dress,
have stayed virgin. It is
a kind of faithfulness.

v

In autumn in Bedfordshire—the smoulder
of haws in hedgerows—the feel
of mushrooms easing rootless from damp grass,
tender with creamy peel—the blackberries—
the gum-eyed cows.
A stringy spinster, appalled by distances,
frightened by sows

and piglets nudging blindly for tits
and the enormous quiet of nights,
I was pleased timidly in autumn by
colours and ripe fruits (feel juice
now in my mouth).
But in every field, and every day, I asked
where was south

and thought of my London under bombs
that quiet weather, how sirens sent
in long spirals, in dowdy light,
my Londoners down echoing steps
while I stood
hearing her say how much like fire and blood
were clouds over the wood.

O she was kind all right. They were all kind—
having us all dumped down on them,
cockney women sneering at their ways,
the kids swearing, wanting fish and chips—
they were a mild
and kind lot, taken all in all.
They always smiled,

spoke slowly to us so we could understand
like missionaries with niggers—and that's how
she treated me, taking me for walks,
pointing out this and that, smiling.
I had to nod,
look grateful, say 'That's nice'. One day
she brought up god

as we stood under the trees among the smells
we'd scuffed up walking, under
a racket of birds. She'd picked wild flowers
and I held them for her like a nana.
What could I do,
standing there with flowers stuck in my fist,
but say I loved god too?

She'd wanted a kid, and she'd got me,
a spinster, 40, who'd had T.B.
thinned to six scrawny stone,
who cried for home like a kid.
At night she'd come to my bed
with hot milk and quiet words
and tell me what Christ said.

But I was lost. She didn't know how lost,
how I'd sit watching trains pass
straight as a dart for London, moan
for the cats I'd had put down, for
my Ada in Northampton,
and for planes
to drone this way, reducing her, Christ,
cows, pigs to flames.

vi

The hospital. I learnt about brain and nerves.
I cried when rain
reminisced. Seeing
leaves bounce with it, sway; hearing
distant cars squirt
firmly over it—it was
a widening of heart

and I cried that it was all
simple, and that I would forget.
At night, darkness got up like a wind,
pushed me from anchor.
It's the brain, I said, the brain.
When I sweated it helped, or when
I bit my lips to get pain.

Learnt I couldn't go mad. Scream
I might scream for the brain to crack,
let in the dark, swamp me. Learnt
it couldn't. Then why give me
a spoon to eat bread
on harmless plates?
It was my head

where manoeuvres swept and clashed.
My hands were innocent. Always
I watched them. They stayed
faithful, could have sewn seams,
cut cheese into cubes, forked
meat. Similarly my legs
surprised me and walked.

This was the way back, separation.
At last I wanted a fork
more than sanity, my cats
more than a lost simplicity.
And that's
enough for starting home with:
love of a fork and two cats.

from INTERIOR (1969)

SMUGGLERS' ROUTE

The journey seems devious—
the route never declares its purpose,
sidling by dry-stone walls. An eye
watching it from a legal window
sees a few yards blotched with moss
abrupt between two corners. Walking it,
with the strain tender at the shin, the
lurch of the breathing body unremitting,
you know this is pure economy—each turn,
each rise, most sensitively contoured
to the briefest way to safety—behind,
the customs-officers, the guilty sea,
before, the whispered sanctuary of the inn.
Push a stone behind you. It will roll
as down a groove until a final leap
clatters it to the beach. Now picturesque,
and the men that scrambled on it glamorous,
this was a desperate scurry, scored upon
a midnight world by burdens of fear and greed.
The need was brutal that made such brevity.
A man was shot here. He plunged backwards, taking
a scream grown legendary, clutching still
as he hit the sea a cask he had smuggled from it.

TRINKET BOX

Tonight, as our child sleeps, you spill
Onto the table from a faded box delicate
Girl-things, long-neglected. I pause
Awkward at work. Your act
Is maidenly. It banishes.

I recognize no habit. Your eyes
Are wholly bright with the presence of trinkets.
Over a tarnished brooch your fingers
Isolate clasp and curve with touch
So innocent, so wonderingly reserved,

I think of how a foal, just dropped,
Nudges, shivers from, nudges again
The sudden earth, its membranes
Fresh, still focusing. You have
No memory. We have not touched

Except the time you all at once recall
By fastening that bracelet to your wrist,
Pale turquoise, a young girl's favourite colour,
And look towards me across seven years,
A memory lying cold against your flesh.

IN A UNIVERSITY LIBRARY

Of all the myths and might-have-beens
I yearn most for the scholar's horn-rimmed stoop
over books so winnowed of flesh, so parched,
that words are precise as maiden aunts, a
bony geometry imposed on doubt.

And my veins cry out for academic blood.
It can turn a body into a college quad
with its grave pacing, pacing. It can make
a brain as steady as the Greenwich clock—
no thumbscrews of five minutes, no lost hours.

So here I am, game for another try.
Across hushed floors I follow appropriate rules—
check catalogues, use cards, go straight to a shelf,
extract one book with unambiguous hand,
pass girls with gentle faces and lyric hair

without a second glance, become a bulk
of silence at a table, open the words—
and Time leaps cartwheels and the blood runs loutish
as sunlight strokes the pages where they swell
in sumptuous buttocky mounds from the shadowed spine.

A GIRL'S WORDS

a sequence on Japanese themes

1.

For him, it was a night well-spent;
for him, it was another bed left cooling;
but I haunt the docks
pestered by sailors.
I only see how quick a ship can vanish,
how fog can tumble upon a bay and heart.

2.

I am seventeen. You have made me shameless.
I see your swagger, your strutting return.
I accost you in the street. All I can say
is Remember me Remember me. The sailors laugh.
I cry because you do not laugh.

3.

Those nights! Worlds
shrank to his pillow.
My pillow now
is salt with sweat, bitter with tears.
I torture it with my nails, as once
I seared his back, his back sweet with my tears!

4.

I'll come. I'll find excuse.
You'll see a shadow
flitting among the willows.
They will think it is the furtive moon.
You will know it is arms and lips.

5.

Gently, love, gently!
My father prizes me like a fragile vase.
He warns me. Tells me he could smell a man upon me.
And reckless you gnaw my neck for the world to see!
Let them!
As for my father, I can learn
to groom my hair in cunning coils and waves.

6.

I moan into the dark, the empty dark,
but I am wise:
a man is flesh, and I've grown greedy for it;
the best are wanderers; their hearts are ships
that launch them into fog, towards new islands.

from AT THE ZOO

Chi-Chi

This is the panda that wouldn't be shagged!
Cages away, you can see the nudging crowd
and the wondering kids hoisted like periscopes.
Closer, you see the gawping envious
wives, flustered by their mistakes, a kid
hawked on to a hip, their legs and skirts
in a quicksand of others. This is the girl
who would have none of it, who let the world
proclaim and plan the grandest wedding for her,
who travelled in state and with due coyness
one thousand miles in a beribboned crate,
who ate well at the reception, honoured the ritual,
and when the time arrived for being shagged
chose otherwise, rolled over, went to sleep.

Here we stand, in our twosomes threesomes fivesomes,
wondering how she dared, and how she can
in public view, in this gorgeous spinster's apartment,
sprawl with such brazen ease in the sensual sun.

SIX POEMS ON THEMES FROM LORCA

1

Cock-crow from the distant villages
scrapes like a blade of light against the darkness.

Where she lies, the spell already broken,
her naked shoulders like a smouldering metal
glow on the ice-white linen.

Already she moves among us, seeking,
across huge plains of daylight, seeking.
And we question 'Where do you go? What do you seek?
Beyond your house are villages, then fields
cluttered with woods and brambles, and beyond,
ultimately, a bitter and restless sea
where to journey is to drown.'

Already she stands
remote from his bed, lust in her loins
dried like his last night's seed. She studies
her body pacing the hours from room to room.

'Wash' says a voice she knows.
'Brush your black hair. Braid it against insanity.'

2

The orange-tree has been an age dead.
It bore leaf when times were legendary.
Its fruit was wild and free as the blood of gods.

Now it is wholly outcry: silver-dead
branches are echoes in green corridors;
they fling outwards, an appalled shout.

No one fells it. It was random growth.
The place of orange-trees is an orange-grove.
No tender axe will free it where it stands.

3

How all that green moves—
boisterous as puppies trees
tumble down the Spring
soft-tongued and eager—on the banks of streams
green sprawls—green gallivants in mud—
in the lap of the sky green fumbles.

The air is drenched green—
it billows across the garden
too vast for the garden only—it spreads
through lives I cannot see, over the plains—
it grazes the green waves—
it proclaims distance.

Death is protean also.
See where it starts, in
the famished orange-tree.
It adjusts itself into a narrowed branch;
a trunk leprous-silver,
an iron root.

4

To lie to him was voluptuous—
to return his stare,
to tell him slowly, never a lid flickering,
'I am unmarried'—it was the body
trembling again, a sudden flow of memory.

And in the grove
I removed my petticoats
starched tight as hides, and felt at last
the cold shock of the world, the living
grass against my limbs.

And then his body
reared between me and the sky, killed
the moon, obliterated stars,
descended huge upon me, lavish
and tender, because I was unmarried.

5

                  And now the sun
          is clamped like a golden beast
      in the steel teeth of the sky. There is
        no progress westward. Shadows
                     will never

                  spill like water
         darkly over this garden where
the flowers stand fixed in fulness, where
      the lime even, that bundle of
                       nerves, is

                  stunned. Here
           in this room always I
embroider eternally the eternal
        moment. Silent fold
                 and fold

                    of linen
                falls like the same
            fold stained minutely crimson
                veined meagre green
                    fold after

                    fold. The
                rigid flowers fill the
        same fold timelessly falling from
            the chained hand like
                    one cry.

6

Do you see her? She is young and leggy.
At her side bounces a child's tambourine.
When she stops far out in the hills her fingers
patter a husky rhythm and the bells ring.
Then she bounds forward, and in her wake the wind
whisks up leaves and grasses, and moans
like a man in love among the rocks.

Look at her—she has played and run
secretly, while you were self-absorbed.
See how brightness lingers in her eye, how quick
she scurfs her hair back into braids, her breast
subsiding. And that is the very wind
that howls in fury at your windows, snaps
mouthfuls of tiles, and will not let you speak.

A WIFE'S TALE

Prologue

I know the tales:
killed on a gibbet
a man walks these hills
under the great span of The Plough
protesting his two centuries' innocence.
Huge figure, howling down

on this tiny city fervently ablaze,
myth of protest, gigantic legendary,
cry for me, exclaim against
this world of lawns, deny
this shapely city
pat in its valley.

Cry for me. I know
how the crowd closed on you, jerked
you choking into the wind. When
at night his hands
slide from my loosened hair, stroking my neck,
I know how the single soul

dies for a ritual. Maintain
shouts that grope the night,
crook-neck, broken illustrious body,
keep your single torture
vital above me upon the hill
crying against the crowd, the unshakable crowd.

1

An innuendo of leaves
was a face today, eyeing
those parts of me; a patch
of shadow, fractionally remote,
whitened with hands—O body,
aching with touch, its memory!

Tonight, he stands
blatant in firelight.
I am his search.
Him I can watch, quizzical,
oddly intrigued,
centuries out of reach.

2

With cripples and the shabbily distressed
I seek this reading-room. I mingle with
these lost in visions, stranded from
demands of daylight, courtesies,
and ritual fervours. One man croons
his pleasure to an atlas, another holds
the world still on a page he never turns.
I grow like these. My visits linger

remembering a schoolgirl, from whose shoulder
my satchel hangs. She waits in winter dusk
fretting a random book in a library corner
for the fated meeting with her only lover—
and all my years of love and children,
the complex ills of feverish nights, the sweat
and hidden crying simplify to this—
a place among the pitiful, a tawdry dream.

3

With dawn they come. As birds
hazard the first frail songs, the door
bursts open, launching
children, their soft bodies nuzzling
deep between us, voices high
with news, although the world is seconds old.
The pale pure light, the birds
rapt in the starting moment, children
with eyes quite flawless—O now I could
be tender to you. Now I could start again,
and risk an arm across you, dare
lean to your sudden face with the first kiss—
I wait. Trembling to kiss, I wait—

until they tumble from us, and the far
ancient world coughs with a starting car.

4

I walk into a trance. I walk
a numb purpose into the brain.
I walk a tired safety from the nerve.
I walk the world small.

From this waiting platform, rails
rise up at distance, float.
I walk the length. Repeat the day's objective:
one journey, one visit, one journey back.
Sun nails the nerve. I talk myself to sleep.
I talk the world small.

A trolley creaks. The nerve tightens, fears.
I walk a drumming silence into me.
I talk me into safety. Wheels and rails
will carry carry. I need not function.
Thought can ease off. Wheels and rails
will cart me like the parcels of that trolley.
Wheels and rails will bring me back.
Sleep is my purpose. Time will take me there.
In nine hours I will close my eyes again.
In nine hours another day is won.
Wheels will carry. Rehearsed speech
will shelter all my visit. Simply walk
these last waiting minutes. After these
wheels will carry, speech will carry,
time will carry. Sleep will carry.
Tomorrow brings its own wheels. Tomorrow
other rails will glide me towards sleep.

Walk into a trance. Walk
just one purpose into the brain.
Walk a tired safety from the nerve.
Walk the world small.

5

I enter, undetectable, all disguise.
Steered by the host, I slip from group to group
eased by the sheer and standard noises.
Faces
blossom around me, uniform with wine.
Featureless music chloroforms the air.

I adjust my speech. And they adjust response.
We know enough of others' histories
to ritualize concern and sympathy.
Our eyes
meet to punctuate, never once
to waver, to imply a need.

And if one now should fail to take a cue,
dislocate pattern, leave my reflex words
heavy in silence; if one should reply
with words that snag, delay—
would I be capable?
Now that you counter with a pause

all I've rehearsed, what is there left to say?
You are the novelty I feared would tread
abruptly through the trance that lasts and kills.
You detect dread
that checks all energies and turns to stone
all smile and gesture. Suddenly, in this room,

we share a silence. All my decent poise
and years of grooming fail, and what remains
is need, blatant and piteous. I
hesitate.
My last words hang in void. Your eyes
search like a hand. And I am recognized.

6

Love, as the world begins
its slow contraction to this room of yours
and the hooded lamp above the bed
heaps light upon your pillow, and our heads
draw to each other, let my random words
in all their waywardness be praise
that what was lost has been by you restored:

the body now grown capable again,
the groin that moistens, and the hands
that reach involuntary upon your limbs.

But when you enter me, the cry
will not be blind—the fingers on your back,
anxious with pleasure, will be tightening on
you only, who had power enough to break
the long enchantment in which my caress
becomes spasmodic chafing, willed, abrupt.
The world grows small around us, will become
two outcries in a darkness—but believe
the working shape beneath you is at last
living again, and knows by whom it lives.

7

My body thrives in your hands:
by mirror I assess
all your voice enumerates
in murmurs over my face—
the skin at ease, the throat
a pulse of content breath,
hair kindled for you, loose,
gentling the oval braced
for years, afraid to give—

But seek out the eyes. I cannot avoid the eyes—
those pupils black, black with immeasurable depth,
they stun like the glimpsed void between stars,
expressionless. Something cannot be changed.
It is this I bring you. It is this I brought to him.
O love, it hungers, cancerous,
perpetual. Hold me. Cherish what has flowered by you.
Linger upon what pulses, breathes, responds.
Still the eyes challenge. It is there
the failure starts—deep, deep,
deeper than ever love has bruised or deadened.

Epilogue

On this hilltop, in the
total silence of the snow, I tell
the story of the suffering
the walking of the hanged man.
Tell of his patrol through centuries,
outraged, faithful to innocence.
Dead. Still walking.

This white waste, high
over the lost town, how it
extinguishes, leaving only
some words in a steam of breath,
spoken by no-one, hanging.
Soft bite of shoes
munches the snow. Turning,

I trace two progresses,
firm and together. I know
you have not heard. The white ahead
is featureless, except here
where birds have patted marks—
landed here, for a few yards
pitted the waste with momentary purpose

then, with the merest surface scuffle,
risen. The snow resumes.
All that has passed here will be softly
smothered—the deep thrusts of
our heels, birds' gentler agitation.
But he will walk, leaving never a mark,
his cry echoing in valleys, in dead hearts.

INTERIOR

(on a painting by de Hooch)

This is her corner. See
the footstool, the low nursing-chair,
the favoured drying herbs, extending
fragrance to the region. She
suckles her child, her breast
bulged by the pushing mouth, her face
a world, half-lighted, half in shadow;

and, round her, the orbit
of wholesome dignities—a towel
casually eternal on a chair,
earthenware pots, sun-contented,
great plaited loaves displayed
like chunks of autumn on a shelf—
the whole, a tribute from the artist-husband,

but more—a harmony whose elements
are the fears and glories of extended love:
above her humdrum pose is set
a crystal vase, singing with light,
a persisting unsoiled splendour; and by
the window, where the spacious Dutch day beats,
a linnet, in a simply-fashioned cage.

from FOR MAD MARY (1974)

from AT VARYKINO

GARDENING SUNDAY

She brushes her hair out in the sun.
This could be a young girl—such absorption,

and the lifted forearm plumped. All day
we have moved together through roses, currants,

silently. Now she tucks up like a girl
on the kitchen step, gathering on her hair

the dwindling lustre of this Sunday
while I wash hands and make the tea for her.

The jars stand full of fruit. People spend
their fifty years going no farther.

CHOPPING WOOD

to think that all of thirty years
brought us here
all its mistakes all that seemed its triumphs
to become on a particular day

a man a woman and a child
in a snowfield in a region far from rumour
on a kind of moon
all that sobbing laughing
to become a way of looking at wood
to become a way of chopping wood
chopping wood and looking at it fly

FOR CATHY, ON GOING TO TURN OUT HER LIGHT

Climbing the stairs, mid-ocean blue,
I enter your room like entering an event:

dolls lopsided against walls, attired
in fancy-dress, blind-drunk with startling hair;
plasticine blob-men from a nordic dream
crawling over the waste-white of a desk;
mother's fifties' flouncy petticoats
and gold dance shoes, careless after the Ball;
a three-ply paper beach-hat, splodged with roses;
a chessman laid to sleep in a three-inch cradle,
his crowned head soft on tissue; four dolls
learning to read; a landscape pieced from felt
with a flock of sheep scissored from a napkin.

My dreams are secret, footpadding through darkness
for fear the day arrest them. You scatter
dreams through the world and let them take their chance.
You sleep now, with the bedside lamp still glaring,
knowing your dolls still read, your gold shoes dance.

THE LANE

Last night, the moon close and touchable,
so richly yellow.
Now, late afternoon,
it ghosts the sky like melting ice.
We scrunch the lane.

He stands, eating.
His eyes slide to fix us when we pass.

Abrupt, we turn.
A cling of briars
gives to a track anciently rutted.
The tut-tut-tut begins
of his blades whittling the next excess.

The pressure of your hand in my hand:
small round warmth, a charm
pressed into a grip.

'AT THE LANE'S END'

At the lane's end
she turned. She did not return.
The unique word
choked on a breath.

Wind veers. Blue poised
on air-stems
vanishes.

Your hand just so,
your mouth thus,
the happenings of your voice.

There are alternatives.

4.10

She gathers her son from school in a white Ford.
Her competent reversing provokes a tender sexuality,
an attractive woman unconsciously in control.
She wears cream slacks, Katherine Hepburn vintage.
Her buttocks begin the slump towards age
pear-heavy, like plastic bags weighted with water.
Beside her as she leaves, her little round-faced son
sits squat and self-contained, a ticking bomb.
She smiles at me as she passes, raises a hand,
assured that I have dealt with him. He will not go off.

from *CREDITS*

STALLED

Counting back from the crossing-gates—
thirteen people taking about a hundred
yards. All engines off: pathetic but diligent
ecologists who can do no more.
After the train had smacked through at ninety
dead empty with all lights blazing
and the keeper like an old-fashioned man
with a pride in his work had scampered
down steps and let us through full pelt
it was clear one woman would not get started
not in our time there. Assuming
an engine stalled or something broken
we indicated, pulled out, passed her.
Only later, recalling
the small hand like a white rag
up at the mouth and the eyes riveted ahead
did it occur to me as it obviously occurred
to others judging by the fluttering brakelights
that not the car had broken, but the woman.

CLOUD

Two days two nights the sky's rushed westward
clearing and has not cleared:
fathomless the origin of cloud.
Admitting the ludicrousness of skimming
'The Celebration of Awareness'
in a damp house with children smouldering
and furious there's no Walt Disney
quoi faire?
At least, I think, we all apprehend
the gist. The dog, called Flossie
for her shambling and shaggy refusal
to be aristocratic,
sets the hall ringing with a querulous edge
Virginia Woolf would not despise.
It clearly doesn't take much bared nerve
to feel the intolerable: observe
the whiskies and the cars heading for Wales.

RELICS FOR A BIOGRAPHY

1

Memories of sensation: she straddled
me, wrenched the cock-stem and its fungus head,

till it sank wet, shapeless, like a rot of undergrowth.
Sun and insects crawled upon us as we lay.

2

Urban sentimentalities: wheels
gulping white miles to the sea

or murmuring through aqueous lanes, splashing green,
burrowing into dreams of landscape.

3

Reflex kindnesses and codes: dutiful
among the smiles and, where the tuts

might shrivel my balls with fear, reluctant;
engaged in transfers of deeds, motoring deals.

4

Morning crosses the creatured farms
waking these things. The wall-eyed beasts

moon in their daylight darkness. On heat,
they moan. The seasons beat their backs.

THE COURTENAY PLAY

Programme Notes

'Sir William Courtenay (as he styled himself to the credulous villagers) was in reality one John Nichols Tom, the son of a Cornish innkeeper. Of striking appearance and feeble mind, he had spent some time in a lunatic asylum before standing for Parliament as a member for Canterbury. The more sophisticated electors of the city would have none of him, but preaching that he was the Messiah he attracted quite a following in the parishes of Boughton, Selling and particularly in Hernhill. His evil influence upon simple village folk soon came to the notice of the civil authorities and some breaches of the law were sufficient for the magistrates to issue a warrant for his arrest. The man sent to apprehend him was shot dead by Courtenay at point blank range. An explosive situation was reached and this caused the magistrates to resort to military intervention. Courtenay and his band of fanatics resisted the soldiers in Bossenden Wood. Eight of Courtenay's followers, including himself, were killed during this battle while one officer and a special constable from Faversham were lost on the other side. There was scarcely a Hernhill family not involved in the disaster: husbands, sons, fathers or brothers had either died in support of Courtenay or been killed in the effort to resist him. The bodies of the dead were buried in Hernhill churchyard ...'

The Church and Parish of Hernhill

'The generally good standard of living of Boughton and Hernhill strongly impressed an outside, independent observer of very good credentials. This was a Mr Liardet, a barrister-at-law, who in July 1838, as a result of the Bossenden tragedy, was commissioned to make a detailed report on the neighbourhood to the Central Society of Education.'

Battle in Bossenden Wood by P.G. Rogers

'The silence that shrouds these village revolutions was not quite unbroken, but the cry that disturbed it is like a noise that breaks for a moment on the night, and then dies away.'

The Village Labourer by J. L. & B. Hammond

Act One

i

Easiest, beginning with them dead.
In life they marched behind a loaf of bread
raised on a pole. Now earth
hoists placards out of their heads

and scabs of lichen
clog the slogans of their names:
chiselled selves
that stone slowly reclaims.

But they are coming, look,
across a farmyard years deep
with dung and hardened
by a bright dry Spring,

in line, hooded with sacks,
a hand of each clutching the cloth in front,
coming like the walking wounded,
blind, who scuffed the Menin Road,

or the mummers, aping the darkness of the damned,
while pipes and fiddles howled
the music of lost souls to villagers
glutted after harvest under the moon.

Soldiers in flaring red
usher them to the barn.
And we have parked
our Fords and crossed the yard

to sit where a bullied farmer
clears the bales. Soon
the Sergeant will unhood the pain.
This is fringe theatre. And has always been.

ii

We apologise. We have no real actors.
We saw their last performance,
remember?
        From their cart they took
a trellis, and the one child of the troupe
thickened and greened its diamonds
with nearby wild rose, and hammered it home on a mound
brightened with daises.
From the cart, with conscious state,
in ancient preserved costumes, stepped the lovers,
down wooden steps, like very gods
thoughtlessly descending in their love
to stroll our earth.
        Our men, who had gathered
for war when trumpets blew, and hurried when
a cow bellowed from a ditch, struggling in calf,
and our women, whom every cottage noise
called from their silent moments, and our children
accustomed already to the beck and call
of fields that would shrink slowly as they aged,
approached and stood.
        Irrelevant sweet words
crossed and recrossed the woven trellis,
ushering the long past back, moments
we had let slip with a grunt or a sigh.
We felt cheated, knowing only the language
to curse and buy with. Later, a man
with lath sword, whose helmet flashed in the sun,
destroyed the dragon with nobility.
We had been taught swords.
That night there was drunkenness. The heroine
was fucked by a cowman in full moonlight on a grave.
Vicar and constable combined to warn them

not to return, and the baked roads gave no sign
the next day of the route they had taken.
We had noticed, anyway, how the steel tyres
slipped on the felloes. The spokes would shake and loosen
from the elm stock. Their cart would fail them.
A year would see it crumbling in a field.

Edward Curling, aged sixteen, hedgecutter,
had heard of dreams, but his night was a black box;
had heard of words, but listened all day to whispers
of a blade against a hedge. And the hedge was lanes-long.
He is entering to perform for you, hooded with sack.
When Courtenay came and on Boughton Hill
sidled against the sun on a horse from Revelations
and sent words bowling down the hill like stones,
that night Curling dreamed. And next day joined the troupe
that travelled through lanes of Dargate, Waterham, Graveney,
and set up plays on the unploughed edge of fields,
in farmyards, water-meadows, wherever labourers
stood silent as their crops or slouched like cattle.
And in Bossenden Wood he raised a sword as real
as any script he'd learned from Courtenay.
He is not dead yet. You can watch him perform.

iii

I came through Dagenham, a Sunday in Spring.
The streets were lined with Fords, and men
lay like lovers on the bonnets, stroking the shine,
or beneath the vile parts, releasing
black flows of pus, or grunted to ease free nuts,
or shone the fixed grins of grilles, or passed
rags over the unwondering eyes of headlamps.
Behind its wire the factory was still, brooding
on Fords yet to be born, emerging
rigid and bright from the hands of Ford men.
Ford men need no sack over the head.
They polish the shine of their slightly outmoded Fords.

iv

You will not see Courtenay.
A tap-cloth covers his loins.
In three days he will be going green in places,
and the Dover Road will be studded with little stalls
selling vials of Courtenay blood, and relics—
crumbs of the very loaf, splinters of the true
staff his hands still clutched as he tumbled on dead
leaves in Bossenden Wood. Unlike his followers,
he will lose his name. He will become
the Cornishman, John Tom. When stones are slammed
clean-cut into the earth above the dead,
his rigid, comically named remains
will be slid into a hole against a wall
in Hernhill churchyard. They will fill the hole
and bang the soil flat. Cut him no stone.
Like all good authors, he disappears,
falls silent as the greatest question is posed,
and the play goes on, and the characters must suffer.
Most lives implode to a name cut on a stone.
Great lives smash outward in a million pieces
leaving no singular trace, only the altered
faces of the shocked, and the garnered
spurious relics of academies, or a heart
embalmed for a hundred years, or burnt like an offering
on a foreign beach.

These nine, who have not died yet,
stretched in front of you, hooded,
awaiting the curtain up,
Edward Wraight,
Edward his son,
Mr Hadlow,
Mistress Hadlow,

Thomas Mears,
Sarah Culver,
William Wills,
Thomas Griggs,
young Curling,
do not yet know there is no more script to learn.
The staff is buried.
On a scrubbed table in the Red Lion Inn
Courtenay lies dead and naked.

v

Ford rolls soft, rubbering gravel
upon clay. Ford
dreams its possessor. I am a Ford's dream.

Door swings on greased weight.
Legs ease out. Ford's sleekness
heals with door's clunk.

Follow the script. Choose the key. Turn it.
World smiles in its sleep.
I am world's dream.

Fog keeps distance all the way,
backs at my footpace towards the wood,
introduces a field rubbled with furrows.

Come on, says the fog. Here is the stream they crossed.
Cross it on this causeway of dead leaves
whose rot yields ankle-deep

but will see you over. Here is Bossenden Wood.
Map says how small it is:
two lanes cram timbers to a wedge

along which soldiers
draw their red cord.
This is their place. Wait,

as hedgecutters, cowmen, cowmen's wives
wait, knowing a three-days' march
meant for them a name cut clean on stone.

Lanes dreamed them. Fields dreamed them.
Cattle and pigs dreamed them.
In the dark of the cottage at night, dark dreamed them.

Now the dream snaps. The red coats
thicken among the branches.
Listen: the wood weeps,

gathering tons of water from the air.
Drops ripen on the tips of twigs,
burn with momentary light, and fall

with the thud of raindrops through the ruined
roof of a ruined house.
Swords free eight men into their names

and a soldier becomes a cathedral plaque
with dozens who died for Empire far away.
Return to Ford. The Sergeant begins the play.

Act Two

i

A soldier's lantern swings the only light.
Our faces flicker
like worlds down corridors of space and time.
Huge beams strut the upper darkness.
Beyond, planets and stars
whirl on their tethers.

In a universe where nothing is forgotten,
nothing lost,
the Sergeant approaches Sarah Culver.

Five red-coat soldiers
ring her, like fingers already bloodied.
One finger moves,
directing Mears to stand before her.
The Sergeant is taking her hand,
placing it on Mears.

'Who is this?
Bitch who could describe the gates of heaven
so the pearls dazzled.
Who is this?'

'I do not know.'

The Sergeant is striking Mears down, dragging him up,
placing her hand again upon his body.

'Who is this?
Cow who stood beside Courtenay, making
madness real, the new world real.
Who is this?'

'I do not know.'

The Sergeant is striking Mears down again, dragging him up,
placing her hand on his body, in his groin.

'Who is this?'

She is caryatid-straight, and weeping.

The Sergeant is smashing her hand up, into Mears' balls.
He is whipping the sack from their heads. They must look.

'Woman who could describe the gates of heaven,
man who marched through lanes leading to heaven,
you have arrived.'

Faces, stars, flicker in their black void.
Nothing is forgotten, nothing lost.
In some world, the Sergeant approaches Sarah.

ii

Thomas Griggs, who would not attend
Hernhill Church 'because there was no glory',
lies like a toppled tree
but whimpering. He is maggoted with pain.
A simple exercise:
face down, hands locked behind the head,
on a trampled floor, with any of five
drawn bayonets ready to jab the spine.
Performed for half an hour.

He becomes lungs.
He becomes shoulderblades.
He is neck. He is point of chin.
He is cartilage of a nose.
He is jut of bone at the hip.
He is soft bottom rib.

Glory?
Fall on your knees on slabs worn to comfort
and pray for ease of this pain and of that,
pray for the flushing of the stone
and the dispersal of goitre,
pray for the loosening of the elbow
and for the usual pains of birth,
pray for an easeful taking of the next breath
and easeful taking of the next step,

for thoughts come and go in their season
and desires shrivel like the last leaves of the wood
and intentions fade like starlight and are as far

but the maggot steadily nuzzles for the nerve
and bayonets
lean towards you, and need never be removed.

iii

The Ford man dreams.
Flat on his back, the globe of his sight darkened,
he sees galaxies of passing Fords, bright undersides,
cars sidereally bright, nebulae
crossing his heavens. He can reach
and touch a star and rivet it in place.
This is privilege. And when one passes,
the gap of appalling black is momentary
as another wheels its shine up and swallows the void.

Count sheep to fall asleep. Count Fords
to sleep like the dead.
He wakes,
and there in the dawn street his own Ford waiting,
god made metal, to bear him warmly
to the Ford factory, where he will lie
watching galaxies by daylight, fitting stars.

iv

Liardet enters, soft-foot.
Here is the theme, quiet and firm
after cacophony. Here is the star.

Courtenay's wild effulgence
is now broken light in these nine faces.
His spent energy dulls to green on an inn-table.

Here is the other light, the official man,
the light of barely-earth-dusted bright boots
and chill shine of the case carrying instructions

from which, flapped like a flatfish onto a bale
falls the other script.
For they have stamina, the official men,

outlasting the wild lights. Their metabolism
ticks slowly, on just the warm side of death.
Living long, they watch season follow season,

hear aspirations clatter round their ears
like Atlantic storms beating the night with fury
and know that every morning comes up good.

They enter on the edge of an event,
slide into the back pew as the priest is possessed by tongues
and begins his utterance that only flames will quench.

They join the drinking-circle as the indiscreet
next round is downed. They step inside the barn
as religious Thomas Griggs begins his wail

for mercy, admitting he is all flesh.
There must be sense. There must be perspective.
This entry takes us. We recall

worlds turning coolly beyond this darkness,
and watch from the distant stars of remembered wisdom
this suddenly small and barn-held recurrence of whispers.

v

Edward Wraight:
                  here I make my statement:
labourer: to Mr Liardet asked but freely
willingly given knowing to be this day
among deaths: deaths of friends and guilty
of death to others knowing and freely saying:
knowing to be punished is what I must and
right and wanting that only that guilt
to be punished and that other things should not
but be understood of me first and then others
so freely made this statement although among
friends hurt and powerful men my enemies
such that I cannot calmly for I am both
fearful here and unused at all tell
a slow account like a building of brick

proof against the storming of righteous men
around my body which must die but only that
one time when to Sittingbourne we came
walking westward and seeing far off
the sun make colours in the dust floating
where gravel-diggers worked: to find
how men can work under a rainbow being still
bent backs as if under a goad although no-one
by still hacking on and through:
no bars free air between us but at our words
gibbering and uneasy in their grey world stooping
and handfuls of grey scooping and with awkwardness
of muscles stiff with other work chucking wild
muck handfuls of it so I could see men in skins
just men barely men in grey skins in their
holes in hillsides frightened to be approached
and at night they fucked suddenly and blind under
a sky they did not understand and the children
came like accidental miracles for poverty suffering
skulking on the earth sharp illness
and lucky meaningless glory: so to call
men brothers Mr Liardet such men all men
is hard and easier to point the gun and blow
the face away Mr Liardet and that you know
and easier going your own way watching the walking deaths
pile up and pile the whole world graveyards and the ways
of men so many deaths: until I turned seeing
my own son by my side and Sir William who has
no son but seeks souls silent ready to go:
and the strength of man is having not souls but sons
for sons must go where you have not gone:
and I have walked some lanes of Kent and come

to Sittingbourne and can no further:
                                        a man's mind stays
where the great moment threw it like a tide
and there unless great other waters wash it
withers and is the bitterness of face
and wound of words no woman's love or weariness
of toil makes sweet or heals: I am
at Sittingbourne: will wither: too soon in time
too wildly in my life came that high tide:
my son here with me and no other son
for voyaging: you take nothing but is withered:
give only and I thank you time for my words:
a testament in a barn and before soldiers.

vi

In my parlour sir for years a large
clock walked and I came to hear its large
foot go nowhere and watch the one
last face of my father I as a girl drew
memory like a hand drawing now
half the lines:
                what did I
Mistress Hadlow have? Or reading there
my three books to myself.
Therefore I let come sir six
unlettered children earth I remember
in their hair their eyes bleaching already
like hedge-hung cloths their gawky
legs all ways on my family chairs
to push across slates their slow
letters: baby-pictures: things they know:
U a horseshoe ready for the hoof

L a flail propped against a wall
A an oust-house top with a cross-beam
easiest of all
O a nothing an empty eye
the way the moon stares through the sky
and sending them sir to find in fields
alphabet like a ghost: N
hid like a riddle in a barred gate
Y proclaimed by a dead tree: so each
morning across my table slid
the twenty six bent wires and sticks
and crooked farm ware that spell
horizons gibberish nightmares kiss
memories love-words: until
one morning sir I give the sweetest
present I have given ever the shape
of each their names: remember
they had glimpsed their faces
hovering on windows at night a
fleeting visitation of themselves: and saw
staring faces from the still reaches
of rivers until wind shattered them: but
never such mirrors as my slates where not
faces but names: names scraped on stones:
dignity like churchyard dead
laid in long rows: how quiet I
remember then my room where six
children watched their names and my clock walked.
Tell me sir where such
things end?
We wrote apple-trees and implements
weekdays and dishes

sun and moon and sheep and fire
brick and earth and father:
time waited: the clock walked:
the parlour window showed long blue
where God sat and souls basked:
slates with names grow empty:
through a long winter the objects grow:
bored: what more do bent sticks do:
is it power used for tricks only
as once visiting jugglers spun
red balls and hid
pigeons in quick invisibility
on summer nights while behind them grew
the ancient unresolved
mystery of darkness gathering
over copse and cornfield and folded sheep:

Sir William came with the Spring:

if I should lie forever as I stand
now here in a cruel darkness
punished that I should pursue
things forbidden unobtainable
shall I blame the innocent
eyes of watching children
their slates filled with lives
their gaze steadily full of me?

Interval and Prelude

I've stopped poetry—
all those dreams.
I always was too dependent:
that little-girl act: those big eyes.
In the States, back there,
we're so exposed—
the darkling plain crap.
We make poetry like we make martinis:
the killed end of the day.

Her kitchen worries me stiff—
so surgically suspicious!
White cold tops of things awaiting a flow of blood:
gadgets that scream into action:
the calendar frozen: she never turns it:
when the dog dragged a bone there, she threw a fit!

I could have died the next morning, driving back through Dagenham
I mean the play had been so … you know what I mean …
and here we were, rather here *they* were … the sense of distance
you understand insuperable. I remembered those four
white figures advancing hand in hand across a white
lawn towards us the audience … and those words …
'Why then we are awake.' The frisson! The obvious challenge …
'Are *you* awake' is what they were really asking …
so that being disgorged into a London street … well, you
can imagine. And next morning still enriched
and *opened* as it were by the whole experience …
to drive past those … those … there are no words …
heads down in the engines of Fords! And that awful factory!
I said at the time, this is a circle of hell
we've entered, and these are lost souls … you can imagine.

O the analyst has me coping:

after all, when she sleeps now I manage as I can.
My body still gathers like a waterdrop
for fall, but I stay as water can't!
Vaulty places like a church—I have really
to hang on there: my legs
like hawsers being cut I could rise
expand and burst. I know—
metaphors—but isn't that how we fear?
Sometimes in the office I dial the time still—
sitting there, listening to time pass:
survival tricks: the way I use the sun
for boiling brains and stunning the nerve:
a moon like this
still worries me—that white gape,
that soundless song.
I'm a sucker for legends.
But it's this trying so hard, and getting nowhere—
I'm not sure I can take that long.

Well you play the game, don't you?
It's all ladders, and you just climb.
And then the end of ladders.
The consolation
is that we know that coast so well.
When it was years ago we took a cottage there
right on the beach—yes, would you believe it—
and the sand stacked behind it by the wind.
The sea was so high somehow:
at night, was it ships or stars that passed?
I've given them the best years—
the old old story.
They've put me out to grass now, let's be frank.
But we know that coast, and that is good luck.
Right on the beach we were:

we spent whole hours and never said a word.
From silence, through the noise of all my life,
and back to silence.
Did one think it could be ever otherwise?

Through all that silence, the sense of fall grows nearer.
The night pays back the day: the hand that stole
through pages throbs like a starfish on the causeway
at springtide: the black rain crackles your lung
that tightened for speech and vented staleness:
the legs that passed between business and business
now with no business suffer under the sheets.
The world must ache and find a body.
Only at dawn as birds transfer
what living is to cadences and exaltation
the body walks from sentry-go and sleeps.
Your dreams are corridors
down which you pass, black-clothed and in hundreds.
What have you done that it should be otherwise?
Where have you been that a different place should want you?
The seasons pass.
The chestnuts split white wombs. Fruit shrivels.
Families open the woodland paths in March.
The sound is down as bodies moan and bleed.
Trees are toppled: a gaunt skyline comes clearer.
The silence is a window on all these.
Through all that silence, the sense of fall grows nearer.

Act Three

i

We are settled now. We purr
like Fords run-in.
Our vision frosts with gin
against the torturer's lamp.

Now we can plump like cushions
round the fist of any cry.
Outside, Fords are grouped like cattle,
their sleek hides gather pearls from the sky.

We survive all fantasies.
The play drips like a candle
towards its dark.
The big door starts its shut between this

century and that, and then the small
doors and the hatches, until with luck
night will close down with kisses
between two faces, and a fuck

between the last places
reserved for contact on our maps.
Liardet approaches, with words
like brandies on a tray:

'Ladies, gentlemen, may I explain …'
It is the third act of the play.
The soldiers ring the nine again
like a last blood-seep round a scab.

ii

... since you are from an age which makes
its imperfections a universal condition,
worrying about foundations, while
aspirations were my age's concern.
Driving from here, as you will soon be doing,
out of the farmyard, turning your cars
for London, you will pass the moonlit bulk
of Dunkirk Church. My report
was instrumental in that building, as it was
in the decision to carve from Hernhill parish
one smaller, more manageable. You see,
we made assertions while you seek causes.
We are, thereby, perhaps liable to the charge
of hypocrisy, whereas your fault
is timidity based on the cult of self.
My age was instrumental: yours conditional.
Hoisting a great brick tower above the heads
of ignorant labourers appears to me
a civilising necessity. Similarly,
my pride is that my report was one
of many that shaped a school system for all:
I stressed the need for schools as safeguards
against superstition, against the exploitation,
for instance, by a man who knew Revelations,
of a populace with a smattering of Bible knowledge
and no instilled discretion. In this
you have lost conviction: again
waking at night from a dream of loneliness,
feeling the universe mocking blackly your mind,
you cannot credit a system based on certainty,
feel guilty, even, when your child goes off to school
compulsorily! You speak of indoctrination,
although such freedom as you find

runs from you at night in sweat, and makes your cities
echo with howls like a forest where man
never raised a home. Such freedom
is imprisonment for me.
                        You perhaps object
to the suffering you've seen here—for those
who are only bodies, bodily pain
is the worst evil—I myself
would shrink from inflicting pain, but do not jib
at having it inflicted as one way
by which my civilisation defines itself.
People are varied in their propensities:
I do not have to be the torturer: the soldier
is conspicuous in red: we know
what to expect from him, the work he does.
My age lacks the refinements of torture
invented by you. We have not, for instance,
faced Sarah Culver with the possibility
that her unused loins have dreamed a glory
round Courtenay's head, and that, indeed,
Courtenay's head may be his cock.
Hadlow was broken, but for *false* glory,
not for his sense of glory. In this we differ.
We would leave the big words, like towers over the heads.
I know, too, that William Wills is January
to his wife's May—think how you would use
such knowledge.
                   I see this occurrence—
this loss of life and blood just fifty miles
from, I dare call it, the centre of the world—
as a warning to my age: these villages
have long had banished from them dreams of joy:
Sundays are bleak: the travelling fairs

are hounded by authority, do not return.
This incident is like a travelling play
devised by people deprived of actors,
minstrels, jugglers; a medieval play
carted down lanes where others had brought plays,
until the distinction blurred between dream and life.
A theatre is the place for plays—a barn like this,
in simple terms, prevents plays slopping over.
When you leave, you will know precisely
where you have been—the cold air will strike you,
as it will the actors, who first
will have stripped their beards off and washed clean the paint.
Dreams, then, must be contained.
The Church contains them, and a well-run school,
and a theatre with seats, and a play performed by others
who pick their props up and go on their way.
You may call this, if you wish, 'bread and circuses'
but bread and circuses is your philosophy,
and *all* of it, whereas for me
it is a way by which unhelpful elements
are calmed, and confusion is unravelled:
in the dark of Dunkirk Church, under the voice
of a well-taught minister, men are controlled, perhaps,
but the church has a tower to take men's eyes
above the fields they work or lanes they walk in.
I wish men good, you see, and know what good is—
freedom from wild and personal dreams
that lead to bloodshed or to unquiet nights.
You have not seen Courtenay because, of course,
he is the fretful personal dream
of each of these nine people. He has no shape

any more than fever has a shape. But you see me.
In my dark suit with boots well shone,
with my unequivocal briefcase and sheaf of notes,
like the church tower I am visible and hard,
dreamless myself, and causing dreams in no-one
but reminding them of strength and certainty—
the great world fifty miles along a road
richer by far than their restless hallucinations.
If these men are deported, or should die,
they will know at least, at last, from what strength
they have been exiled. It is less hard
to die knowing of certainty.
Ladies, gentlemen, we confront each other tonight
for a brief moment across a century.
Let me admit, I pity you your exile:
I see you pitched suddenly on some shore
with a dwindling memory of continents.
Pity is for the lost. Whatever your response
you cannot pity me, and can do little
but pity these nine. You see in these your forebears:
carting their fevers through a web of ways
and ending homeless in some black barn, or the hulk
of a pitching ship on an unfamiliar sea.
When faced with them,
I can speak words of comfort or rebuke.
Meeting these nine as equals, you
find nothing to say,
leaving them as you found them: which means worse.

iii

Liardet's sad masques for our time

Four men raise
a white-draped mound from an inn-table:
he is really dead:
like a log rotting he is slid straight
into earth: earth covers him without stone:
earth grows its grasses: earth is dreaming:
four men scrub
the inn-table: a live man lies there:
his head is a helmet of wires: he arches
in a blue crackle: he sits up like a doll:
four white men smile: tears
pour like a doll's tears pulseless:
he gives his new name without tremor:
he asks for food with perfect grammar.

She is eating eggs
as if it were a profession.
She is watching a Welsh lake.
Three car-seats are empty.
She weeps and bites the blue-white of an egg.
She switches the wipers on
as if her tears were a squall from the lake.
She has come three hundred miles
and will stay two weeks.
She has a Welsh phrase-book and a Welsh name.
She loves the gorse so much she weeps.
She has tasted rowanberries for their bitterness.
The brown bag is greasy and full of shell.
She must write a postcard to someone at home.
She cannot sleep at night
in that loft of an old farm.

She has forgotten so much and carries wads of maps.
An old stone stands like a hitch-hiker.
She weeps because it has already survived her.
Intrigued, she counts the keys on her keyring.
She counts the one lock on the dashboard.
She opens the roar of the engine,
drives weeping away.
The lake stirs and throws a wet
battering wind
down a road empty but for a stone.
Here are two sailed into quiet haven.
Each is the other's sole achievement.
When she sleeps, he sees images of death,
and where he once bent kissing, bends to hear
her next breath, her next breath, her next breath.
She shines the bowl of a spoon
once more. He is late for dinner.
It is a slow grave dance they perform together.
They hope to bow and curtsey to each other
and sit down together in the danceless room.

iv

Going: the whole caboose shunted off into the wings.
The moment when the actor moves a suddenly different hand,
and the hired farmer straightens the bales like farmwork.
With a shock, we are suddenly
dramatic, awaiting our own next move.
Little coughs tut tut and then the hands
break open a drowning rain washing the stage
really clean like a thankful child
releasing the black of his slate

with a wet rag. Come back, say the hands,
come back different and smiling. But this time
nothing: their century is finally
closing and on the bright side of those doors
we must pick up our coats like another
burden altogether and with those we love
or have merely come with step out of the barn
to an empty farmyard fierce with a Spring moon
noticing no footmarks in the dust.
Edward Wraight and Sarah Culver and teacher Hadlow
will not come smiling to the party afterwards
their faces scraped pink and their hair
with a fine white dust at the root.
Far as stars they are so absent.
The soundless open mouth of Griggs screaming
has reached a distant planet, is passing on.
Across the universe eternally we will pursue
his agony with our suave
wretchedness always a century behind.
The tempest subsides. Liardet
frees his Sergeant for other work.
We pray not to arrive
at our own black island
the moment when a life burns to a focus
so luminously perfected it must end.
Their graveyards wait. They are already there.
Or the moving spot in the ocean. Or the scattering wind.
While finding the Ford's key, look up. We know
the death our century promises: bodies suited
in brilliant padding: faces shadowed with visors:
in silence that still receives and still gives way:
fast as a bullet: stock still with not arriving:
dead as we lived: forever further away.

from

THE SPITFIRE ON THE NORTHERN LINE (1975)

For
STEVE *and* CATHY

THE SPITFIRE ON THE NORTHERN LINE

Harry was an uncle. I saw him twice.
Both times he was a sailor home from war.
First, he arrived one morning, thumped the door,
Annoying old Ma Brown on the second floor,
And brought me two string-bags click-full of marbles.
In the grey light of that wartime dawn we lay
On the cold lino, rumbling zig-zag balls
Of colour to all corners of the room,
Until Ma Brown banged up at us with her broom.
I felt like a god in heaven, playing with thunder.
The second time, we went by Underground
To see his mother, my grandma. In all
That packed and rocking tube-train, down we sat
Together on the dirty wooden slats
Between the feet of passengers, and began
To build a Spitfire. He would send me off
Toddling with tininess against the sway
Of the train to fetch a propeller, then the wheels,
While like a Buddha crosslegged, all in blue,
He sat and bashed a nail or sank a screw.
And before the eyes of all, a Spitfire grew
And finally (a stop before the Angel)
He cried 'It's finished!' and the whole coachful
Shouted 'Hooray!'
          Never, never again
Did I see Harry. Somewhere he was killed
And they slipped his body softly to the sea.
Thousands died that war. Most, like Harry,
Not distinguished by the enemies gunned down,
But remembered by some child.
                    I see it still,
That Spitfire on the Northern Line, nose-up,
Blotched with its camouflage, and gleaming bright,
And all those faces laughing with delight.

BLUEBELLS

Forest is brief
On a day such as that was, and I took
To gloom gratefully, and to the quick, dank smell
That waits years for the scuffing of a heel
To set it free. I knew behind each leaf
Lurked the emphatic sun I'd wearied of.

The trees straggled
And I prepared for heat, when suddenly
I came upon the bluebells, endlessly
Discoverable, like stars the eye can will
From darkness, until the darkness is all stars.
Hint joined with fleck, fleck broadened to blue swill

And I stopped
In water-freshened air, my nostrils wide
And temples doused. It was when I bent beside
That generous wet, and singled a blue drop
To cool my palm, I saw that withering had begun
Out of some weariness not due to sun.

from THE ISLAND NORMAL (1980)

from I. THE ISLAND NORMAL

'… place your hands on the sources of its ugliness …'
                                              Kropotkin

OVERNIGHT

Stopping somewhere in England at a place
nondescript, halfway to our intention,
we get a bed and garage the hot car,
lugging only the one white case upstairs
to a room we barely look at.
We eat what's here and pass no comment—
it's chance after all that we've alighted
between the poles of choice.
                              But look at her face
who carries plates to us and responds
to what must be a child howling somewhere
in whatever part is private in this house.
She also is smiling since it doesn't matter
but going from the room has all the swift
compulsion of the really trapped.
We glimpse again all those momentous wheres
we're always absent from, as when
the train unscheduled stops, or the tyre
flattens in an irrelevant street. But not
tonight the normal rate of jettison.
Later we lie actually studying a room—
someone's taste of paper and curtaining, someone's
odd aside of a landscape, raw, unframed;
restlessly sleepless on futile snags of question
who have come in from the night to feel exclusion.

THE ISLAND NORMAL

So often we push off from it, bored stiff
by its rightness, taking ages to jettison
the blue prescription of its near-shore waters,
and in no time we know we've insufficient
stomach for the great swell, and our bark
is far from noble, and should we both
flop and disappear, few will remember, fewer mourn.
It's the getting back that's miraculous—
it's really miraculous: chartless, inept,
working only at the next swell, the next buffet of wind,
we're hopeless. Then up it heaves, the Island,
as if unanchored and full of compassion.
Back over that bay, its blues suddenly gorgeous,
stepping on to the jetty, the wood creaking,
we're primed, it feels, like Odysseus with marvels.
But since we've been nowhere, precisely Nowhere,
of all those quiet Normalists, who shore-based know
the obvious horrors of ocean, who will listen?

TOO LATE

All those old crap songs poking their heads
round the blind alleys we walk and wringing
the nearest thing to tears from these dry hearts.
The air of putrefaction when the bar raises
its Sunday voice in 'I'll take you home again
Kathleen' and we all wanting to drape our arms
round everybody's neck and say 'yes, that's how …'
and waking with gritty head on Monday reading
another child is dead with his plastic gun.
Forgive our trespasses. We have many trespasses.
We're all doing our worst down the wrong
road, and the crap songs like Little Nell's foul death
jerk our sickness weepy. Sirens are calling us,
miles-away, long-sailed-past, long-refused.
Achilles shagged Penthesilea when she was dead.
Rightly, we feel revulsion. We understand.

END OF PIER

Its abrupt angled indifference to coast
took the mind's breath away,
though bright-as-paint lay soldiers oompahed
on it, and an enthusiast's midget train
took you nowhere and back. The turnstile
thwacked your bum as you entered, vulgar
as the tatty comic turns. The rickety
slot machines flickered Edwardian porn
or, never converted, thrust out hopeless tongues
for ancient big brown pennies. Down it
you quitted Sunday afternoons
for a sky like Hollywood
with your first sweetheart. Below, fathoms of fear
merely licked the tree-trunk legs. A float

bobbed. A weighted line hissed endlessly
aimed at the horizon.
                        First, the fewer
people. Then paint peeling
from unprofitable arcades. Then three supports
gorged by the sea in one night of storm.
Then the fire, and this calcined skeleton
seen at first light nibbled into the sky.
Only inland is left. We watch the notices
nailed up: how it's forbidden to walk
now towards the sun, or strut the sea.
A small 'if only'
has gone, a yearning, a huddled
discreet town's V sign at itself.

RETURN TO WASTEGROUND

A patina of fuel on half-size marguerites
and a Volvo showroom with a launching party:
wide-lapelled young men, their raspberry
and mustard wool ties tumescently knotted: the wives
nuzzling older influentials with their uplifts.
Once I stood here in a fair among limping
fairground music watching a ferris wheel
mine couple after couple from the dark earth
and saw a fox skulk among perimeter diesels,
slung low like a lizard between its shoulderblades
expecting hurt. Country on the edge of town
means we are coming. First the fox goes,
then the fair. The only cause for return
now is a Volvo. A sheer and satiny one
stands like a celebrity no one dare approach
at the heart of the party. It cuts me dead
front on with its blank and armoured face.

THE SLAUGHTERHOUSE FOREMAN'S SON

The slaughterhouse became the abattoir
when my promoted father took to suits
and no longer in the evening brought back home
that cold hollow smell of opened animals
or fingernails delicately rimmed with blood—
coincident with my entering grammar school
noosed in a black and silver tie and hobbled
with itching grey socks to the knee. On Sundays
we walked stiffly together in our new success
and have never since that time said what we thought.
I relate, however, to those departing cows
munching at mud as if it were lush pasture
in the paltry acre attached to the windowless
square building, towards which when it's time
they're led, nodding yes yes to their fate.

THE SLAUGHTERHOUSE FOREMAN'S DAUGHTER

I can't forget the ice of his returning
kiss or the touch that slammed the bolt.
When he drew his belt in a notch
it was a prelude to hauling carcases.
My friends seem to have no jobs.
My lovers shower and become real with a scotch.
When he carved meat, our table was silent.
My friends are words. He was hands.
In his anger he loomed in a blind room.
His caress drew my head swooningly back.

THE SLAUGHTERHOUSE FOREMAN'S WIFE

The heads lie till last,
he told me. Complete and watching.

The opened bodies I see them travel
wide and red as screams
losing the lapped kidneys
the livers bruised as afterbirths
while those perfect heads
gaze and gaze.

Only then the uprooting of tongues.
The scoop-out of brains that understood.

A SLAUGHTERER WATCHES

That brewery swallows coachloads whole
and spews them two hours later, pissed.
Floury barley, wrinkled dry
baked opiate-sweet hops, magical
sideshow vats of creeping yeast—
a tour of wholesomeness and splendours
ending in wayside pukes and hangovers.

If they came here, I'd make them leave clear-eyed,
with a dripping hunk, choppers, knives
and a bolted gun: process and product
indivisibly one.
Nobody visits. My children crawl
on graves for schoolwork, waxing dates and skulls
to decorate bedrooms.
I kiss them goodnight with work-chilled lips
and never stop to talk them off to sleep.

FEARFUL

I'm a Romantic—it's just this unaccountable
agoraphobia that holds me back.
I'm a natural for footloose
speculation and shouldered haversack—

the expedition of one
among mistresses and orchids
though my whole sense of travel
is of life on the skids

plodding from chair to set
varying the channels
irked by endless reading
of minuscule novels

Why does space hate me?
The trigger somewhere and the finger curled.
When I was a child and real I lay
on our tar roof and itched for the world.

MARCH THE TWENTY-FIRST

All the returning images. Farmsteads
glowing like old-brick braziers. A sumptuous cat
homed to a hot-spot, dozing. Cattle
crossing a field with that yes-yes of heads
as if earth murmured and they agreed.
We gather the brittle hazel the storms
long past shed, and later by the fire
remember walking the same lanes years ago.
Your hands smell of bark-flakes. Your hair
holds wood-smoke like a deliberate glamour.
To have strolled
so much nearer loss of each other

down lanes so little changed but for
that knowledge leaves me lying
hearing your deep sleep breathe
like steps departing, imagining
insupportable Springs—the wood-smoke
uncaptured, my mouth to kiss it gone.

IN MEMORY: E.S.

What kind of death is this we have to mourn?
For when I think of her I cannot mourn.
When lost in London, gripping her railings,
I wept and muttered This is the end
she opened her fusty backroom for me to sleep
and hung my jacket up and made me laugh.

She made us laugh when dutiful and taut
with dutiful taut family I visited her.
One night I dreamt of her and woke up laughing.
When relatives spoke of her it was with laughter.
When they shut her up in a ward she had them laughing.
And now a small cortege creeps through the streets

she never left, and we look out seriously
on the battered houses she would not recognise
and the ones they've tarted with amnesiac white.
An old man stops and lifts his hat among
the crowd, and I thank him; and three children
to our amazement cross themselves and stand still.

Old warehouses blind with corrugated iron,
the road where she was born reduced to rubble,
her school a private house with BOYS and GIRLS
ghostly and chipped maintained as talking points.
And everywhere those bland discredited heights
stacked with people winkled out before her

who stuck like a last root in her basement flat
and would not go and died when they unearthed her.
What kind of deaths are these we have to mourn?
Old forms, old houses, old civilities;
three children's semaphore that no one soon
will comprehend? In dribbling music the unseen

fire turns you to ashes. You would have laughed,
laughed at the gibberish on the well-thumbed pages.
I cannot mourn for you, for you lived well.
Caged in your history and your class's history
you made the bars ring with your jaunty cheek
and cocky irreverence. I stand, and grip the railings,

gazing down. The door you opened for me is planked across.
Dead ice-plants shrivel against the boarded panes.
The first-floor workmen already smash the walls.
Bless you—forgive the word. Thank you for everything.
Old atheist-hypochondriac-anarchist, who knew
the world was crazy, embodied it, and laughed.

ON THE EDGE

The arsehole of England. Muffled birdwatchers
squint through tears of windy joy—
ecstasy a puffball on stilts. A school
of local artists—acrylics and airless realisms—
endure the wonder of their admirers.
Remittance defectives, the trepanned crazed,
the obsessives abandoned to their treadmills,
line the seawall, blank as Aunt Sallys.
The Victorian towns crumble their piecrust
derivative splendours and are losing trade.
Decisions are made here. The word 'future'
bandied as if it were an option.

II. AENEAS AND AFTER

Constitit et lacrimans 'quis iam locus' inquit 'Achate,
Quae regio in terris nostri non plena laboris?'

HORACE BIDS FAREWELL TO VERGIL   Odes I.iii

I trust. friend, you appreciate
the nervous cost to one who hates
the sea and loves late drink
of standing on the brink

while your unnecessary boat
drifts fainter in a queasy float
into liver-spotted mist.
A poet who's half-pissed

and whose tool and wit are frozen
can't deliver a few well-chosen
words, sublime or droll.
Vergil, you're half my soul

torn from me with slow pincers, but
just now it feels like half my gut.
And I know the signs: slow
sways the sea, no winds blow,

it's that dreadful act of balance which
the sea-god plays before his fits.
To trust a mind like yours
to canvas, rope and oars

and to sailors more hung-over
than I! O I see with horror
the nibbling fishes eat
you, anonymous meat!

I hold it truth a man with brains
should keep his hat on when it rains
avoid excessive sun
walk when the world says run,

and here you are, a luminary,
behaving like one supernumerary!
How will this fraught world fare
if poets, devil-may-care,

put everything at risk, like fools?
Poets, of all men, should know the rules.
How life is cobweb-frail,
to be spun where no gale

shakes it. How highest-fliers flop.
How hope evaporates like a dew-drop.
What most men learn with groans
poets know in their bones.

A poet's life and art should be
twin warriors against extremity.
(Excess of love and wine
permitted: both supine

in their aims, enjoyed at home,
they're free of the Icarus-syndrome.)
This urge to be away
when wisdom says stay

bodes ill both for your life and art.
The mist smells cruel. The salt is smart.
The blank sky has received
you wholly. I'm bereaved

and die your death. A double hurt.
O wandering soul, come safe to port.
And may we meet again
and drink and smile, and when

we exchange work, may your new verses
triumphantly mock my prognosis
and tell of one who found
home good, and tilled his ground.

AENEAS

1

A father prophetic among the dead
spells out the politics
of my inheritance. A wife
cries 'It is finished!' A palace
roars behind her like a hearth
grotesquely magnified. The lost
loved faces. The walled
city among its fields. My arms
encircle nothing and dare not let go.
Only
the burnt-out past is real. I move
on through sadness like wading water.

2

All point away. Tide and wind and prow.
And fate, in me reduced to history.
On watering-place islands
our fires of dead wood
sink rapidly to ash. 'Every fall'
I tell them 'is the future hoisting sail.
Lop the best trees to mast the ships
as the gods lopped Troy!'

3

Failure clings to us like a tradition.
A steersman overboard
welters from beach to beach.
My dreams hatch his cries for burial.
Every morning I must see to it
that my face comes up from bad dreams like the sun.

4 *At Carthage*

I come in out of horror to this warm bed.
Her thick gold hair murders the endless blue.
The sweet salt of her shoulder
is what the capricious ocean can shrink to.

When gods leave, fate pales to obligation—
a few sour colleagues waiting with twiddled thumbs—
somebody's book aren't straight—some letters
lie unopened—stocks are run down—a hand drums.

She does it properly. Her bed's exalted,
cornered with pillars, curtained with purple gloom.
Quickened with gratitude, I'm fully up to

the expectations of this sealed-off room.

At dawn, I wake alone. Are they still waiting?
Is that ship safe, banging against the quay?
Are we provided? Is that sail patched? Are
these the new gods—Detail? Banality?

5 *The Site of Rome*

A plain. Some mountains round.
A slowed river leaves silt.
A sow under the alders farrows
fulfilling prophecy.

The conspiracy of signs!
All this backslapping
and grins above the wine.
As if anguish ever earned

a simple future, and gods
grew never bored.
I bow my head
and whet stone a dull lance

expecting any time
a distant assembling clangour
our first harvest of packed
and hostile metal

at whose head
a young prince rides
so familiar: fierce
with love of country

who cannot countenance
thought of defeat or exile
whose wife waits in a walled
city for the only outcome.

Him I must track down
and with a joyous
savagery, that leaves my soldiers
stunned, nail and despoil.

AENEAS CONSIDERS THE TRIBES

I see these ancient fools worship their gods:
the one of gold dished in a roaring blue,
the other silver with a gaping mouth
singing in silence in a black surround.

Their opposition makes of one world two.
One god must fade before the other grows.
Allegiance cannot tolerate that both
reign unconcerned above a patch of ground.

My journeys are all sea in groans of wood.
Lucky the tiny islands, the hot coasts.
Lucky my journey should it come to good
poised over rocks. Beneath, always, the ghosts

crying from unshaped darkness far from land
claimed by quite other than the god they chose.
Our temples must house all gods, and to raise
them, men with ocean-tempered minds.

ON

There was one spoke of another journey:
the whole mistake
of keels pushed over shingle
into the blind sea

and squabbles about a new name.
Daily they watched him
farther and farther off
in that quietening corner of the room.

FIRSTFOOT

A shadow figure walked
into the wood beyond the settlement.

Behind, the deep drowse
of their first sleep

the bottles scattered
glinting like eyes

the start of walls
jagged against firelight.

The wood explored him.
He heard songs

die like a species
a crumbling silence of handiwork

the resentful slither of undergrowth
into the egg of another silence.

On the plains of the pitch black
the unkilled emerged gorging the unburied.

He felt himself
driven inward like a nail.

FIRSTFRUIT

At dawn
the women of the conquered

ringed the settlement.
By next dawn

the future had found its womb.
Delighted by relief
and a clutch of new tricks

the men

hewed rooftrees
and planked the sky.

PRESENCE

He heard another in the room.
The click of ankle-bones,

air through particular lips.
He knew he was himself alone.

He screwed the vice close every day.
But he heard another in the room.

TO SLEEP

He travelled to the beached ships
to scuttle nostalgia, the sweet dreams.

He saw the moving stones digest the planks.
A spine of keel

all that remained of travel.
The dreams ebbed

and he entered the mud-flat
sleep of absence

from which, reeking of landsweat,
he woke again, knowing he had dreamed.

A RELEASE

He fought for years. His body
closed in and tortured him.
The vice stomach. The gnawing genitals.
The ears were singing like a dried kettle.
The lungs cutting the air short.
He awoke from dreams coiled and whimpering.
He thrashed and squirmed and stabbed.
One night he fell. Down through the dreams
that cried for him, down through the roots of dreams.
He sank vanquished through water-table tears,
through the ooze of all decay, through the black
dismembering silence. It was the end
of all importance. Nobody knew
he had been born. The enormous flames
of an exploding planet quenched him painlessly.
It was sweet, sweet. He awoke laughing.

THE DREAM

He stood at the window
as the voice bade him.
He felt the air's affection

and saw sun misted
on a far hill.
A blackbird sang on a shining bough.

A stream trapped
a surprise of light.
Along a track

a man bore a mysterious load
towards a wood
whose trees fused

in darkness.
He closed his eyes
as the voice bade him

and knew the question
before it came. Is this
place dusk or dawn?

UPON CRAPPLETON HOUSE

> *The Beasts are by their Dens exprest* Marvell

1

And now, they said, there must be a Centre.
And they toiled three years.
Those who remembered proportions
drew thin blue plans

by night under cowled lamps.
The hefty wielded pickaxe
and shovel, gouging
troughs through strata.

The rogue toughs churned
mushes of concrete, and the more
precise laid level lines
of brick. And from the ranks

a plasterer came, and a strange
remote man with the secret of glass.
Out of the woods
chimed the strike of axes,

and, tall, fine-fingered, one
ruled and planed and stacked
sweet resinous planks.
Another, finicky, herringboned a floor.

And just as, in a hive
rolls a murmur, confused yet harmonious,
as creatures skilled in one skill
pursue their blind genetic stars

and miraculously the tiny
strictures of self merge
to elaborate concordance,
so the tappings, thuds, chink-chinks,

clanks, squeals and slithers
subsumed themselves at last
into the singing silence of completion.
And they stood back to see that it was good.

2

It was disastrous.
The high-hung concave dish urinals
splashed piss back accurately. The tiles,
pinned arsey-versey,

fell like leaves at the first big wind.
The elaborate concertina-sliding
partition slid once only,
jumped a crooked rail

and fell, scoring irreparably
a floor already found to be
susceptible to hard-soled shoes.
The elegant all-round clerestory,

lacking panes of like dimension,
made impossible the installation
of the cheap blackout required
for the inauguration of film-shows

envisaged to establish
the Centre as a place of pleasure.
The heating system irregularly
launched spasms of percussion

driving away a Yoga class that found
contemplation and the development
of inner harmony impossible
in such conditions.

No door
complied with the half-hour
burning specifications.
No cupboard was large enough.

No vision that they had of man
could be accommodated in
this bleak and bald
reverberating barn,

even the letters of whose name
sunk in a hunk of porage concrete
appeared slowly like slugs
only in rain.

3

Something had crossed
oceans with them,
tougher than nostalgia
or recurrent dreams.

So many leagues of emptiness
travelled, such pain
endured; and still incompetence
flowered from design.

The ashes were cold now
on that distant shore.
For this new beginning
they had come so far

to an earth untrammelled.
The journey stopped here.
And the Centre proclaimed
they had reached Nowhere

to gaze in horror
at their fresh start—
a Centre, sprung crooked
straight from the heart.

III. AT GREAT TEW

'… so that many came thither to study in a better air, finding all the books they could desire in his library and all the persons together whose company they could wish and not find in any other society.'

AT GREAT TEW
thinking of Cary, Viscount Falkland (1610-1643)

'… and would passionately profess that the very agony of the war took his sleep from him and would shortly break his heart. He was weary of the times, he said, but would be out of it ere night.'

i

As he could not heal his country's disease,
he longed for death. Dressing himself cleanly
as one going to a banquet, he drew the flap
and stepped into the tented field. An army
stirred, and small fires through the morning mist
blossomed. A nervous boy
fidgeted fingertips on the war drum.

He stands and gazes. The morning light
gathers like elegance at wrist and neck.
Across an English field he stares
into the mirror of an English field
where small fires blossom.
Between the fields, the dark fume of a hedge,
and a linking gap …

ii

High summer. The Cotswold stone
returns light, softened. Echoes,
echoes everywhere. The lane
tunnelling green through covertures of scents
leads to a mossed and pitted gate, beyond
which, becalmed now like a photograph,
his house stands, at whose table, before friends,
the wine and meat were sanctified
by ideals of moderation, while the candles
glimmered in Oxfordshire darkness, itself
in an England black with storm.
And the storm rose, and each light failed
one by one. No man survives
alone in blackness, can only grasp
whatever is to hand, and that always
is weapons, the simplicity
of alignment, leading inexorably
to a misty field at dawn
before the battle ...

iii

Hooves
gather to thunder over mist-soft earth.
With light fixed in determined eyes
he kicks blood from his horse and pulls ahead
aimed at the mirrored enemy, that gap
clean in the hedge where image coincides
with image and a hail of lead. Comrades
and foes, stunned, rein back to admire
momently this career of death ...

iv

The picnic crumbles, slips into the grass.
The Sunday paper brightly features
'suicide chic', the hagiography
of exemplary failures:
a poet toppling from a bridge,
an aviator heading out to sea.
The tone of commendation and the staring
ikons of centrality sit well
among advertisements which also fail
to mention price and efficacy …

v

The Sunday's camera would have caught it well:
that split astonished second when
two hell-bent forces faltered as there lay
between them a small island of one man;
until one side saw in the death
bravery flowering from a certain cause,
the other, panic from a loss of nerve,

and craning forward, screaming, both came on.

ANDREW MARVELL AWAITS HIS CHARGE

(In 1653, Marvell became tutor to Oliver Cromwell's ward)

The fountain spatters the stone boys.
An endless rainbow dribbles back
To sway the water-lilies. Poise
Is what the drizzling droplets lack

Then gain once more when thrust up high
By artifice to slide the groove
Ordained against this garden's sky.
The rainbow hovers there to prove

Art's function: how it can beget
From wasteful slop of water what
Is glittering yet is not wet.
For art is real and is not.

But art requires a sun. Although,
When clouds form, still the arc remains,
It is as grey as what below
Slips like decay into stone drains.

Blest are those peoples bathed in sun
Of certainties. Their simplest songs
Shine effortlessly and are one.
Eden must be where art belongs.

But now, unless one man can find
Within himself a grove of calm
Some quintessential spot of mind
Beneath disturbance and alarm,

All song will strain but to rehearse
The common wilderness where each
Is wandering alone. But worse.
It will be error granted speech.

About me, flower with flower chimes.
Colours concur. The beds of flowers
Like stanzas intricate with rhymes
Bespeak the quiet gardener's powers

Who constant among springs and falls
Handles each season's energy
Working on wildness between walls
To resurrect a harmony

While at my back an emptiness
Is by design of mortared stone
Shaped like a comfort from distress
To house the smaller house of bone.

For us, who cope with words, who know
The cries of butchered innocents
And how they pray who left them so,
The irony of reticence

Is all the crop we dare produce,
A tiny plot of sheltered green
Now wantonness is on the loose
To trample what is simply seen.

But there is one who spreads his arms
To welcome chaos of the times
Embodying all our alarms
And voicing nightmare without rhymes

Presumption I will not attempt.
My stanzas tremble but not yield.
To versify pride and contempt
Makes art compliant, like Mars' field.

He is a spirit great with powers
But here comes what he cannot see:
A tiny child among the flowers
Reluctantly to learn of me;

A ward of brutal times, and given
Into my charge, the future's seed.
The rainbow dances against heaven.
A covenant has been agreed.

The milkwhite flowers, the flowers red,
Tokens of innocence and pain,
Sway either side of his soft tread.
It is my duty to maintain

A tightrope discipline of mind,
My present to the future which
Approaches, nervous as a hind,
Green fields, or slaughter in a ditch.

from THE CHILDREN OF SEPARATION (1985)

INTRODUCTORY: 1944

1. *Fed and Watered*

Here is my generation. We are ranked in a hall
neat and crammed as sprigs in a seed-box.
Outside, the first harvest we have ever known
is steadily reaped with softly whirring blades
and rabbit squeal and leap through an air
whirled gold. We groan a withheld sensual
ecstasy, yearning to handle ourselves
and each other. And then we sing: *We plough
the fields and scatter . . .* In the aftermath
one of us walks forward and is caned,
the whistling downcurve slicing through the palm
which is severed but does not fall. All our hands
are guilty. Paired, we turn to each other,
fisted, clawed, our mouths wet with desire.

2. *The Attendants*

The June sun blazes, releasing richly from the garden shed
odours of creosote, dead geraniums and paraffin,
and from Mr Greville languorously sensual recall
of afternoons spent there with Mrs Evans, whose body
his hand explored as now it explores the curves and crevices
of his deadbeat sofa. Mrs Greville believes he labours
over a tract on tomatoes, a miracle crop of which
he produced in the summer of nineteen thirty six,
before there was war and evacuees.

He is the backbone of England, working at night to fashion
metal killing-objects in the factory near the canal,
on whose banks he munches sandwiches alone on moonlit nights.
He passes watching homes on his ticking Rudge slow and stately
as the light departs, and they all say 'There goes Mr Greville',
drawing their curtains close, and settling down to hear Big Ben chime,

comforted and unalert, writing no-news to relations,
while elsewhere rise bombers, searchlights and constellations.
At twelve, the London train beats past on time.

Mr Greville knows that life's logic is uneventfulness.
It is luck that throws up wondrous tomatoes, Mrs Evans,
and a trusting wife. Eat big and sleep deep. Do not interfere
with the world, and keep your eyes open for the pickings of chance.
When he wakes in the afternoon he yawns and scratches his crotch,
and on hearing the springs sigh, Mrs Greville prepares the toast.
He knows he is loved and trusted. His hand plunges more deeply
into the sofa as into opportunity.
Today, another war-flung woman comes.

Pauline will grow into a darkly mysterious woman.
Already she has fluttered several hearts among the beet-fields.
She has learned she has power, but has not yet exploited it,
has, instead, a dim mysterious sense of being exploited.
The London boys touched her body like musicians touching strings,
and the music quivered in their cheeks. She did not feel music.
She has learned a thing or two for when another boy arrives.
Among the nettles by the station she keeps her eyes
staring southward. She will not miss a trick.

It is not easy to be teaching, to be alone, teaching,
in the uneventful Midlands, to pass your endless weekends
walking alone among the growing grain, feeling the skin teased,
feeling the prickle of sweat define the raw edge of yearning.
Miss Cowans hates the children with their futures and whisperings,
the way heads sway in assembly conspiratorially,
the way the hands she canes are sticky with out-of-school horrors.
Faces stare back at her like impossible mirrors,
like the faces that face a refugee.

Peter is conspicuous for the sharpness of his dressing—
smart pale slacks, crisp shirts—and a look debonair and masterful.
But no-one understands his feelings, understands why he comes

every week to the station, to sit alone drawing the rails
narrowing into distance their certainty of purpose.
He teaches the wounded in the transit camp, himself wounded
from birth by a withered ankle his fashionable slacks hide.
He knows that after the war there must be a new world.
Lonely students like himself will found it

who are now preparing themselves at night in cocoons of peace
as khaki heroes and demagogues hog bombarded stages
and loom large in the searchlights of simplicity. However,
he needs these weekly visits to where the railway lines run bright
southward to the heart of power, to cities that are waiting
for the arrival of peace, for men of knowledge and vision.
But the lines run two ways. He sits at the heart of arrival.
He yearns to give, but is an empty receptacle
awaiting love, the spur of social passion.

In nineteen eighty three, a train oddly anachronistic—
a lovely slow swayer with softly bouncing seats, corridors,
and windows set in walnut, so that the summer world passes
gradually and in incidents like so many paintings—
rocks towards the Midlands. On board, a man clutches a black case
rich with unhappy poems which he will discharge that evening
guardedly to a scatter of listeners in Nottingham.
He is charmed into smile by this train, its old rhythms,
feeling a deep-set resistance yielding.

He will be lulled by this journey—as a child in mother's arms
drifts in a moving human warmth towards the abandonment
of grief—into a sleep he has not known since he was a child,
to awake stared at by a station and long level grainfields
and by a mother jauntily pretty in a pillbox hat,
who will shepherd him over the slatted wooden bridge towards
vast arrests of feeling, that will hold their shapes like armatures
and gather around themselves unfulfilling futures,
and foul all journeys but the journey backward.

FANCY BREAD

    an elegy

Tell me where is Fancy bred
Or in the heart or in the head?
How begot, how nourished?
    Reply, reply.
It is engendered in the eyes,
With gazing fed; and Fancy dies
In the cradle where it lies.
Let us all sing Fancy's knell:
I'll begin it—Ding, dong, bell.
    Ding, dong, bell.

Song: *The Merchant of Venice*

1.

A teacher flogs a desk with a pitted rule
a yard long. 'Time!' he is yelling. 'Time!'
An imported beauty from the juniors
squeaks a ball-less 'Where is Fancy Bread'
while we ding-dong under red Shakespeares and gaze
wide-eyed and innocent. Only when the song
has ended, and Beauty has simpered off
to jeers and whistles, and the teacher pounds
bum keys on the jangling upright, preserving
a barrel-organ parody of the tune
as though it meant a lot, do we close in,
baying with ecstasy as his fingers sink
a silent note.   We catch him miles away,
force him to wheel, teeth bared, the rule aloft.

2.

That summer. I am lost in unmapped lanes,
lured by music which is England audible
towards an unkempt privet hedge, veined lilac.
And there he sits, jungled in garden, whispering
love-breath to an English flute. His face
is abstract with a young man's softness, all
his fingers, strangely long now, tenderly flutter.
Scarlet runners flaunt extravagant red purses.
Marigolds adore, and spindly cornflowers
bend at him their own weight, like the failure
of all ambition.
                     I would brood now upon violence,
creep quietly away and brood upon violence,
upon Fancy mutilated in its cradle.
The theme pervasive in the dulcet air.

3.

The game has rules and everyone must lose.
We stand in fidgety ranks and hear him dead.
Some are sniggering. A tired headmaster drawls
the unbearable comedy of his all-round skills:
of helping years of first-years learn to swim,
of coaching soccer teams when he was younger,
much younger. A clamped guffaw explodes.
Last, and minimal, words about his music,
about his life. 'His gift was to engender
a love of music in hundreds of young men
or, where he found a love, to nourish it.'
That night, I dream of Fancy Bread: a loaf
plaited and glazed and starred with sugar stars.
In dream, I gorge it, and awake unfed.

AT BADGERS MOUNT

1.

The images that others have of us
sustain and kill. When I left one gallery
twenty years long and found a flaking
caravan flimsy under tapping apple-boughs,
they paused at the broken gate, the walkers,
and coloured my desolation with their eyes—
a bronzed romantic in his peace-camp,
dropped-out and speculative.
Did he feel substantial, too, and wholesome,
the landowner, to see me picturing him
richly hauling a winter's heat from woods
in silvered lengths? And his wife, brooding
earth-motherly over vegetables in the kitchen?
But for all comes night, and its gallery of mirrors.

2.

Hugging the existence of the last voice
on the emptying wavebands, I survey the dozen
closed companions who had no choice
but to come with me: Edward Thomas, Kilvert, Jefferies,
Wordsworth, Cobbett—a whole consolatory
landscape lugged like a creaking set of some
tatty touring repertory to be assembled
in the teeth of desolation. Doctor Johnson,
for when the mad tide rises. Hopkins, for nights
like this one, now the voice has stopped
and the empty singing starts. No end to the shame
of the cultivated man once the sinking has begun
and his sweating hand reaches to choose among
Arnold, Milton, Shakespeare, Mogadon.

3.

The child lies between two women,
a mother and an aunt. In a distant romantic war
a father muses on the desert sifting
between his fingers, and will soon receive
shrapnel in his bronzed left arm. The white
ship waits to receive and transport him home,
a weight to place in a balance that will never
be redressed. The child stares at one
and then the other. And then into before-dawn
darkness, a world all female, where two vixens
dispute the looming wood, and a moon
hints valleys and secrecies. He unlatches
the plywood door and breathes the musky air.
His feet are bare, but he begins to move
up a long slope steadily, like a drawn sea.

4.

Another caravan awaits him in the wood,
a wreck invaded by waves of nettle and briar,
settling into a past. When the moon catches it
as the boughs stir, it is momentarily
where the princess waits in her cocoon of sleep.
When the moon is hidden, it is awash again
and dingily shipping mosses through bulging
ply. Who stayed here? Did another traveller
punctuate his life one former spring
with dreams and desolations as the apples formed?
And when he left, was this caravan
the husk of a fulfilled purpose, or emblem
of all that a life can expect? Indistinguishable now
from green rampage, except when the moon glances.

5.

Across the walls, the watery dawn-light walls,
blurred spread-hand shadows hurtle—the outside birds
orchestrated to fury by the Spring. They zoom
from hedges where nests have swollen like fruit
to lawns where the worms lie glistening to be cropped.
I ache with the grief of dreams, lie coiled
on a conscious shore with dark waves surging still
from oceans that have toyed and finished with me,
where creatures were faced human, clawed and beaked,
and moaned with pleasure as they ripped and ate—
endless waves of centuries of faces
around whose lips were smiles of stinking blood.
Now brutal, guiltless, the shadow wall-birds leap,
remotely real. I climb a shore towards them.

6.

The starlings are slicks of tar shining poured
on the orchard posts. Their throats crawl iridescence
and throb with song like a heart. Dozens of others
run oil over wet grass. So metaphor should be casual
as colloquialism, and the night-presiding dream
be incorporated into the hand opening the plywood
door onto nettles and the cobwebbed milk-path.
Something infinitely precarious about this hour
hazes over the landowner's clear intentions
among the woodpiles. He is flanked by two children
holding yellow flowers, whose purpose seems to be
a presentation of large watchfulness and acceptance.
A promise of red broods in the apple trees
and everywhere is unhurried recognition.

7. Approaching Shoreham

The most intransigent illusion is the good place:
a pair of arms, a cottage by a stream, a lane
to be walked at night towards a lighted window—
if found at last the end to pain and dream.
I think of Palmer's self-portrait, as a blackbird,
oblivious and complete, sings me towards his valley,
how something feminine, suffering, beat at his face
in panic, and fled forever never arriving,
the way on that slope beneath the green of wheat
flee the backs of nervous shoals, flee endlessly.
High on the valley's side come the roadmakers,
a white scar on a green flank. They march
like an army of god, scouring deception. And there
Palmer's moon still rises, the moon he quit to recover.

8. Newsreel

This, with all the unarguable blatant caricature
of a nightmare cartoon, declares I am, we are,
the children of war: women hooking dolls onto barbed wire,
butcher-birds aborting the future, and the primed
silos itching to eject their zero spunk.
Between them, the forlorn police have the look
of stunned revelation: nobody loves them,
they are despised most by those who hired them.
They are designed for small-scale beat-up and backstreet
terrors, not apocalypse and symbol.
Somewhere unseen in this mythic confrontation
a woman hangs not a doll but unfinished knitting
begun for me. In the distance, what we breed best—
a row of military awaiting their time to fruit.

APPROACHING ISLANDS

Your white Madagascar flowered dress,
gift of a censorious elder sister
bespectacled and hairstyled for efficiency,
swings all its flowers across this hillside,
and your smile of disbelief
lights on me as I climb. Your hands grip
oats and marguerites and purple currant.
You are beginning to arrive. Your hands
will place this small and English haul in a white
vase against the window and then in the tall bed
hold me. I too am learning to arrive.
Midnight. Your arms are tightening on an English
coast of flowers and fruit. My face against you
admits a Madagascar of dangerous blooms.

TALKING

Together, as though we had paused in flight
from our own times of danger. You unpack first.
Other people are histories. Ourselves a scatter of snapshots.
Pink the figs burst against the dazzling walls.
The deserted church where you dared God and left disappointed
will crumble no more than then. It is likely that the man
shot in the neck will always be toppling on his knees
towards you, and you a child in a white flowered dress
be the helpless last beautiful thing his eyes see.
Wholeness, perhaps, is the final reserved gift, and he received it.
Meanwhile, in the face of our lovers, we unpack the pieces
and yield to tenderness. This feeling of time stopped, or ousted,
or defeated, may be the approximate wholeness we living
are granted, the future glory of our snapshots.

SNOWMEN

The irony that day, the pure windless one
that always dawns after the night that breeds snow,
to walk perfectly together, hip socketed against hip,
free in love's enclosure, and to witness those gurus
inspecting the world through cinders, their ice-lips
clamped on pipes as though they had reached an unnegotiable
status such as death. All gods are made by innocent
hands and are left dazzling and unapproachable,
crystalline obelisks yearning at the moon.
Successfully, my love, they provoked both relief and guilt.
We had known two people like that, the burnt-out vision,
the agonised dignity beneath inappropriate hats.
And we had known that blinding surrounding emptiness,
that absence of ringing voices, where children had been.

EARTH LANDING

It is the ordinary that shocks, the ordinary
landscape of my new world. The autumn
gorgeously dishevels the chestnut trees
down there along the lane, and the spired white church
is rooted among those yews with frosted berries
like a rocket content never to take off.
I have taken off, and moved with a rocket's
appalling stillness through Nowhere. Now, it seems
I must come to earth among continuing business—
close-order marguerites bright-eyed and stubborn,
some tissue-poppies, bravery on thin stalks.
I pass a tennis court, wet-black with rattling leaves,
and remember people. They are indoors, waiting
for a friendly visit and firelit reminiscence.

A VIEW

The season's rust ranges along these trees.
The pigeons slam off down the wind, pure weight.
High indolent clouds fatten their gold bellies
and trail the hillsides with nonchalant shade.
My mind is free. Our apple-white and honey
tiny flat was a three-months' crucible.
Your love-flame tested me in glow
and would not let me be until I was.
'Come on. Pain must come out. I can take it.'
There's a violent berry-flower startling the hedge
that I struggle to break for you and bring home
and thoughts I must bring home: my daughter
struggling to breathe and sobbing 'I never guessed.'
I watch the road in the valley travel two ways.

OXFORD

We love our children, hate ourselves in them.
Somewhere, perhaps, my son, your secret
iceberg-deep universe that floats daily from me
holds a tiny function to help me forgive myself.
I explode a furious patronising laughter
at your fascist neighbour's door, its tag
odi profanum vulgus et arceo.
You hush me smiling: 'We've found a way
of co-existing. It's mute, precarious.'
This is appeasement, or wisdom. I follow
your gentle figure in Canadian airforce blue
down ancient stairs. I had come to Oxford
to explain parting and the pain of choice.
We have talked exhaustively. Everything but.

THE CHILDREN OF SEPARATION

While waiting for you to come, I imagine you sitting
in a stopped train between stations, feeling
at peace in no-man's-land, where there is no need
to say 'we' or 'our', or 'home', or other impossible words,

where the poppies among the corn
recall distant universal pain
cushioned in history and innocence.
How unusual it must be for you now to enjoy silence,

with no-one to crave your assurance, no-one to grasp
your hands, stare into your face, and guiltily ask
'Are you all right? Are you unhappy? Will you say?'
No-one you must gratify

with tears, or the absence of tears.
Suddenly, you are among the ranks of those
who once seemed as unlikely, as remote,
as the handicapped, the poor, the mad—

the children of separation, those who are given
two Christmases to halve the pain
and find it doubled, those who are more prey
to nostalgia than old men, who have been betrayed

by language and now handle it like bombs,
for whom affection is a thicket of spies, and surnames
amputations with the ache of wholeness.
Every book taken down is inscribed by loving parents,

and albums of photographs refuse to be otherwise.
What can be done with memories?
What remains of the self if everything that was
is now framed in the inverted commas of 'seemed'?

I imagine the brakes sighing to the inevitable,
and the train resuming the purpose of the rails.
Soon you will step out into my story
whose pages for too long I kept closed to you.

We will walk through fields I am still making mine,
and when the time comes for someone to say 'Let's go home'
no-one will say it. On the platform, we will wait to be parted,
your hand clutching a ticket to somewhere rejected.

RETURN JOURNEY

A summer fog mid-Channel. The slowed
engines thrum like a guitar. Long ago
the French gulls veered and disappeared, and all
but we sank to the reassuring bars.

How your eyes totally receive and give!
Your hair is jewelled and salved in the drenched light.
We are so refugee, so prone
to inhabit this halfway stillness of all oceans

where the quit shore and the approaching are unreal,
invisible and undeserved, and only the yes
of each other's face affirms we move, until fog
lifts, and a breathing ocean frees the bows

and on the skyline a quick scratch of chalk
fidgets in lively atoms: England and home,
words that still hang in vacancy as I mouth them
as the daisy blows at the cliff's edge. The final gift

is to look calmly on the surrounding hills
or walls, on the stretch of moderately
worked garden, the past with its approximations,
the future with its death, and to say

'This is mine'—a daunting task for one,
well past forty, still learning how to say
'This is me'. Now silent watchers join us
as the dancing atoms seriously become

a shore, and green hints of inland
with its roads and loves, towns and disasters,
haunt the amnesiac sky. Whatever we have made
awaits us, to pester us for love

the way you pestered me, a weary walker
emerging from a dark lane to find a moon
blazing where I imagined more dark lane,
and would not let me rest in my preference

for darkness. The place we are flying from
is where we are heading. The dream from which we try
to rise, like a waterbird extended shaking wings,
is where we must settle and call home. The shore

subtly becomes a harbour, then a quay. The light
is crystal and undeceived. Arm linked in arm
we sway across slats, and where the land begins
begins the road, inward, returning, and then on.

NO SMALL MURDERS

There are no small murders. One wound
seeds a landscape and smears cities. History
stares you in the face at every turn. When you ask
what hope is there when people like us fail and fail

the answer is already enacted
on the plains of Europe where Europe manoeuvres.
Fists of dust hang like breath in cold air
behind each one of us. It is how we came.

This destruction will not be removed from the earth
by claiming it was our right, or we did not understand.
The swallow returns to skim the green wheat,
the one promise kept to the children,

and to stare down through water is to find in a tiny
rockpool insignificant against the sea
transparencies with legs and the beginnings of colour,
frail alternatives to absence, eating and spawning,

though the sea might never reach here again and the sun
breed its dryness in a twinkling and all be gone.
The future waits beyond a palisade of ghosts
like the idea of calm water on a wind-ruffled day,

simple, and universal, and easily forgotten,
like the taking of offered hands, or offering hands.

from FREEBORN JOHN (1990)

"Ah, I see," said the Inspector. "You have misunderstood me. You are under arrest, certainly, but that need not hinder you going about your business."
Kafka, *The Trial*

For Bill and Ada, my parents
and for the Kinship of Jones

. . . to learn to what extent the effort to think one's own history can free thought from what it silently thinks, and so enable us to think differently.

Foucault, *The Use of Pleasure*

INTRODUCTORY
1638: FREEBORN JOHN

'If people knew the times where they were cast,
they'd look about them:
see the great Squares grown shambles, note
how Execution, flagrantly empowered,

lops ears that hear, melts eyes that see.
The main ignore
the iron in the flesh and soul, twitch down
the brim of fact, and squint the ground.

Close in chambers, men take the oaths
by which they are accused. England
staggers, debauched by Law. Injustice
prowls among the orchard-trees,

serves up the ale, and clinks the wage.
I see honour only among graves,
the stone fleets of the just dead,
the traffic of deceitless bone;

and in him, the one they flogged
from Fleet to pillory, his hands
still showering to the heedless bands
sweet seditious leaves, new-pressed,

till clamped beside his head. His mouth
then cried 'Wake, England!'—till with wadding tamped.
At which—O wonderful—I saw his feet
risk their small liberty to stamp … stamp … stamp.'

STANSTED SONNETS

for my father

1.
At the War Memorial: Autumn 1987

Together like yoked oxen we lean
into this tailgate slam of tempest.
An equal brevity of staunched stride.
A muscular understanding after
lame decades. We have entered the kinship
of Jones: one of the snapped tap-roots
of anonymous names—Betts, Blackman, Bowyer,
—curt mossed laterals, from which flowers
this svelte youth, whose beauty was the profile
insouciantly sought in mirrors
by the generation whose gas its flame
was lit to sweeten. Between spread, raised arms
crackles a leap of frond: Peace,
on which, in our line of sight, he hangs nailed.

2.
The Bronze Figure

His half-stride is that archaic
hesitation towards consciousness.
He broaches the trance of myth and enters
history's squalor, where perennial bronze
bleeds emerald down marble towards
the rising moss, skirting white islands
at the heart of names, pure o's, small complete
moons lapped by a stained sky, an essence
persisting, a bequest of nothing, innocence,
something gone, a moan gusted across meadows,
endless, broken. Flint in wind-skimmed furrows.
Eyes of bone. At the frond's ragged tips
drips black debris, like gouts from legendary
chopped boughs. Insistent sacrifice.

3.
After Hurricane

A stumped timber statuary bleeds
memory down the bleached lanes: Constable's
moist collusive vision, murdered
by the swingeing tail of tempest. Helmeted,
a madam clops her Arab-faced blond mare
fastidiously in a shimmying finesse
of broken boughs. An embalmed
dislocation staggering for poise.
The churchyard wall is breached
to a cold flick of flint. I imagine
outriders of the New Order pausing
to gaze down into the heartlands
of the self-defeated. England's face
truly surfacing. A brutal, frightened stare.

4.
My Father's Faith

Remember Bevan? a haughty blub
of tilted head bobbing on its sibilants
at the cavernous end of a barn. An owl
at bay. The fine contempt of the doomed.
I stood shoulder-to-knee with you
at that by-election. Truth had a start
of eighteen over the ravening pack—
Fear, Loss of Nerve, Self-Interest. Surely
God could swing it! Every night I prayed
to His commonsense—Who could only plump
for the future, and gave his nod
to a watchful dwarf in glasses. You wept,
hearing clipped Atlee's curt goodbye.
God after God packing into the past.

5.
Get-together

When Joneses meet, they embrace in a great
sigh of alignment. They drag a honky-tonk
into a pool of tears and vamp The Gipsy
and Shine on Harvest Moon. Men kiss men
most unEnglishly. Nervous new-Jones spouses
are initiated with reminiscence and huge
scarlet and mauve hearts on the cheek. The dead—
squandered by war, tuberculosis, suicide;
and the six-week-old great aunt, who never
took shape, except in memories—return
in whispered, tearful corners. A powerhouse
throbs in the night—all those clear
unsullied eyes, those springs sudden as truth
welling from bodies bought but not wholly given.

6.
Family Album

A tea-gold face, a several-times great
grandfather, sharp enough to prize
a new contraption that sucks the soul
and sends it purely fading from inessentials
into the future: pale, furious, visionary
eyes, persisting in my eighteen-year-old
virgin grandmother, her winged shoulders and tilted
chin cleaving onward, and in her nut-shrunk
monkey-face, bitter among three children
six years later. An heirloom of unsatisfied
uncompromised requirement, an unblinking
arrogant insistence, of which a distant
uncle was robbed in Flanders, an aunt
died uncured in a house of the mad.

7.
A View from Stansted

A cold vision is settling into place: barbed
certainties that mark red in the balance-sheet
the questioner, the immigrant, the reflective;
it crushes discourse beneath its monologue
and proves dreams pathology; sees us scrabbling
on a dying planet and sneers Why not? Colonised
England wakes to find itself facing itself
in the rigid lines of winners and losers.
Its vaunting irony, its booted curled-lip
humour, its scything realism that takes
every thought at the knee, its trip-wire horror
of all touch except tickle and rape, are coming
home to us down the inevitable lanes
to claim their birthright and to wear our face.

8.

Betts, Blackman, Bowyer, Brown, Briggs,
Green, Jones, Walker: we have been
available as headstones, prompt as fodder;
defused by an Africa Star, a gilt watch,
tits on the breakfast table, and a need
for a V Reg Vauxhall. None but our lovers
wept at our scattered limbs. We kicked
Indians in the stomach, Gatlinged
Zulus, jeered black subtle wingers. We reached
for the juices on dangled hooks, and fuelled
the juggernaut with our blood and choice.
England is posthumous with our fidelity.
We stand among broken trees as Outriders
rev their machines to cruise towards our Yes.

9.

They are coming, father. They have settled
helmets over their brains and kicked
machines to life. They warble across
the tarmac lanes. I want you to start
speaking now. I want you to tell
your story endlessly like a faultless
loop. I want the album open
at the sepia but glaring eyes
of all our generations. As they arrive
to force our door like confident guests,
be there, in that magisterial chair,
a history spread on your lap,
with me, my children, and the framed ghosts
attentive, like drinkers at a source.

from CAESAR'S PROGRESS

*This is your enemies' country which they took
in the small hours an age before you woke*
Geoffrey Hill: *The Mystery of the Charity of Charles Peguy*

The Images of Caesar

So many bald-eyed impostors
gazing down the echoing galleries of the world

all with their advocates:
Stoffels favouring that brutal-jowled

bust in Naples; Nieburger
that green basalt block in Berlin,

narrow-skulled and blunt of vision
(like Nieburger).

Others quite failing to see
how a clamped hysteria

or a louche and fleshy menace
points to Cicero, or Sejanus.

I can only wearily reiterate
'This is the one':

He outstares the changing light
and makes no plea

to be understood, liked, or forgiven.
He has shed blood without remorse

for the sake of some greater good.
His smile plays like a cold sunlight

on the pit of human failings.
I return day after day

and watch for hours
as he yearns savagely through the thickets of time.

Caesar's Progress

No conqueror concerns himself with questions
Of ethnology: the word is no more in
His vocabulary than in a poet's.
Both forge relationships, not acknowledge them.
But we may speculate on what manner of men
Peered through shaggy eyebrows from the rocky heights
As slowly, insensibly, civilization
Moved on, with clank of iron, creak of leather.
Enthusiastic, impulsive, quick-witted,
Childishly inquisitive and credulous,
Joyous in victory, despondent in defeat,
Impatient of law and discipline, they were
Ill-equipped to resist that high-principled
Juggernaut crushing roads of scruple and bone.

The Schooling of the Tribe

They stooped to the yoke, and then arose
With the degraded cunning of the unhanded.
Phlegm laced the lord's sauces.
Piss frothed the ale. They gauged

Their skills to the just-unpunishable.
The guts of their speech rotted with irony.
Manhood proved itself with fists. Women
Starred in ritual humiliations.

Yearly the tribe trekked south
As permitted, along permitted
Roads, for schooling in those dream landscapes
Promised to the full sleep of servitude:

Through sunflower-fields where adoring faces
Lifted as one towards the brazen
Hanging Christs, and poppies and marguerites
Spattered like transfigured blood and tears

The iron roots of the cross. Water-cannon
Like generous, opened arteries
Pumped long glittering ostrich-plumes
To seed the air and haze the lolling

Tongues of maize. In island cemeteries,
Embedded softly in fields like natural groves,
Porcelain petals winked, and chrysanthemums
Smouldered remembered love upon the graves.

Here were a people grappled to verities—
Fruit and gathering and proper dying—
Stooped over fields and graves beneath the sky's yoke,
Free of that savage purity of self-regard

With which the tribe slunk by, poisoned
By memory: the hoarded violence
In children's eyes as they fingered
Bayonets raked from the beet-fields;

The sea-stopped edge of their world
Where curt headstones, lozenge after lozenge,
Stepped off infinitely in bureaucratic
De-creation. Sun, and bulging peppery

Wine would be theirs for a month,
And the lectures of salt-rimed sensuality,
And the amnesia of the raped palate,
From which every autumn they returned

A little more inclined like sunflower-heads
To the sun of the inevitable, to a brutal
Approval of law and order, and to direct
Visitors to the historic war-graves.

Caesar Chooses Leaders from the Tribe

The grudge of tribute. The sloping
Shoulders brooding on rage. The whining
Down-wind voices of the hunched women.
These badged the tribe, became the inheritance

Of the watchful young squatting at the hearth
Raising their eyes from Latin or the plains of History.
Most slammed the books like doors, and mimicked
Slouch at street-corners, and sour-handed work,

Setting up homes where they engaged each other
In speechless violence until both died.
A few made sense of what they read, gathering
Tongues and perspectives. These were rewarded

And watched. Very carefully watched. They rose
Like corks inevitably, until the time
Set for their trial, known as interview.
Here, they were given words to use: Control,

Leadership, Decision-making, Management.
And words to interpret: Negotiation,
Consultation, Team. All were punished.
Some with preferment and the memory

Of wholeness. Some with wholeness and a desk
In a cobwebbed corner of a province. Some
With flogging till they were insensible
And then beheading. Those sent to provinces

Were watched. Very carefully. It was suspected
That they might correspond, or meet each year
Murmuring to one another on a beach under the sun.
They received regularly details of new posts

And dates of interview.

Action Plan from Caesar's Inspectorate

He offers his hands
We chop him at the wrist

He phrases a meaning
We invert it in commas

He sees the situation
We call it paranoia

He falls in love
We maintain it is illegal

He embarks on a search
We publicise his uncertainty

He observes boundaries
We declare him obstructive

He embraces wholeness
We put him on an island

He moves inward
We announce him mad

Application for a Post in Caesar's Bureaucracy

Sir (or Madam), I have the politic
skill that dismantles the true
answers to questions lobbed at me
and returns what you currently
approve. Also, over the years,
I have quite successfully
cut myself in two

which empowers me
to face both ways, smile
in all directions, and not know
if I am coming or going.
No-one believes anything about me
except my power, which is,
of course, yours, sir (or madam).

My 'no' can sound
like 'We'll see' to the strong
and 'Tomorrow' to the insistent.
My cringe is perfectly clear
to all offices on the upper
floor, and their anger
panics me to punish

the weak (for whom I am developing
a ferret-sharp appetite).
My two suits are appropriately
stained at the crotch
and anally, and blotched
on the collar with a steady
fall of hair and scurf.

I learn rolling on my back
from my two dogs,
deception from my children.
My wife's craven inadequacy
teaches me so much

about the needs
and history of women.

I am, of course, not a complete
shit, nor a total yes-man
yet. Somewhere I have anguish
but not too much
and it is not all that important,
sir (or madam). Those I sell
down the river

I do grieve for:
it is always so unnecessary.
It needs only a little bending
this way and that way
and everything can be
as it should be, whatever
that may be.

I intend to put together
a volleyball team
to represent the service.
It is not my fault
if those who cannot
grub or spike are those
we can well do without:

that simply indicates
a deep pattern in things.
I am quite prepared
to offer my counseling
to the inadequate, all we require
is a willingness to learn
what's what, whatever that what is

or what you might
change it to.

I believe in good practice,
but there are many ways
to skin a cat, and who's
to tell who's right
except those whose right

it is to tell us?
I like people who smile
(but not knowing smiles),
buoyant, optimistic people, preferably
women with long crossed legs
who smile most of the time, but know
how to weep when it gets rough.

I can, therefore, affirm
my sadism, my skills
of sycophancy and coat-turning.
My record proves my paranoia,
and my referees are eloquent
testimony to my hollowness
in which orders are echoed with pure

unadulterating accuracy.
I am prepared to move
anywhere at any time
for any purpose.
I feel I am ready now
to shoulder greater burdens
of servitude

and crave the opportunity
of interview.
I once worked for you
but trust you will find me
sufficiently faceless
as to be utterly unrememberable,
sir, (or madam).

Caesar's Circular, after Implementation of the Four Year Plan

Nothing radical has happened.
And in any case it is now all over.
People have a thousand reasons
To be happier and more productive than before.
It is hoped that words like 'buoyant'
And 'optimistic'
Will be found more frequently
In all reports.
People can still meet,
Of course they can.
It is just that records will need to be kept
To facilitate payment of expenses.
As for the malicious rumour
About centralized control—
Well, we are investigating that.
Of course we have confidence in our procedures:
The key appointments were made
By a thrifty greengrocer from the West Province
And a practical mother-of-four
From the East—the sort of people
Who know what's what, and who were voted in
By fifty-one percent of the seventeen percent
Who voted. Those who have disappeared
Received, we can assure you,
Appropriate recompense. The demoted
Will receive counselling in our Retraining Centres
And in time will apply for posts
Like different men and women.
If anyone has any queries or concerns,
Please let me know in writing
Taking care to indicate name, address,
Post code and telephone number,
So that I have no difficulty
In responding at once.

For a Nativity

1.

Every birth is premonitory pang
in Caesar's heart, his fatal flaw.
He curses the legions into double-pace.
His spotlights sweep the barbed compounds.

2.

The animals understand:
something has happened small and shouting
on straw unexpectedly that needs
to be muzzled upright onto its own legs.

3.

A winter event:
frost-seeded furrows,
ice-veins clamping the world's heat,
bloodberries spattering the snow insistently.

4.

There is the pattering of tiny feet:
it is the Imperial Extinguisher
scuttling to every stable in the land
with the official Aims and Objectives.

5.

Birth distils what remains of hope:
the water-drop at which the dam cracks,
the outrider of depths,
the dream that haunts noontide.

LA TRAHISON D'UN CLERC

*Compulsion and enforcement may make a confused mass
of dissembling hypocrites, not a congregation of believers.*
        William Walwyn: *A Whisper in the Ear of Mr Thomas Edwards*

1.

You must know from the outset, I am resolutely
unclubbable. Please do not be-comrade or be-friend
me. I am prompted by Puckishness. I wish to prove
that when Secrecy racks its great presses down
an irresistible sweetness extrudes, drawing
all manner of insects, you being one.

2.

The Chief Executive is wetting himself. He ranges
our dismal corridors howling 'Leaks!' like a deprived
Welshman on Saint David's day, or an indigent plumber.
It is a source of deepest glee for me to disturb
his dreams (where, I am sure, he merely programmes himself
like a good computer, to conduct the reign of terror—
I really cannot imagine him enjoying
a towards-dawn tumescence, although perhaps 'cost-efficient'
throbs and grows quite luminous in the small hours.)
Attached, a memo to the disciplinary think-tank.

3.

Find enclosed a confidential proposal
to sell your buildings, and to loose you down the wind
for market-forces to prey on. I am deeply offended
by the constant mis-use of 'will' for 'shall'
and by the structural absence of the possessive apostrophe.
The latter bespeaks no respect for proper
ownership, and a preference (also exemplified
in the refusal to use full stops with abbreviations)

for unseemly haste, curtailment of courtesies,
and disregard for procedures. Use this document
as you will to wreak the utmost damage.

4.

The Chief Executive sees himself (did he but know it)
as the Vergil of Market Forces, rewriting all our stories
into an epic clarity and persuasiveness; leading the tribe
from a bankrupt homeland (justly in ashes) towards
a cost-efficient new foundation, ringing with Roman virtue.
What I find distasteful is the absence of Vergilian
silvered sadness, the decent trace of tears.

5.

In this paper (which names all those employees
suspected of resisting the new culture, and who
are to be purged in the next review) you will find
a flagrant misuse of terms. Students are called
'customers', and seats of learning 'properties'.
Pursuing this logic, Caveat Emptor should be engraved
on the portal of my old College! Really, my dear,
this might be witty, emanating from a more rounded
gentry, but from the arrivistes who manage
this mutilated province, it amounts to boorish
bullying. Please use your incendiary skills
to fire the thews of hoi polloi and oik.

6.

You will have observed that, on the very day
the KGB produced a promotional video,
PIS (our Public Information Service) launched
its upbeat, demotic tabloid, full of buoyant
zombies. I am outraged. Although the higher echelons
were diplomatically not featured, nevertheless,
in some deep if distasteful way, I am a colleague
of all those smiling faces, the Province's employees,

whose lives this rag distorts to advertisement.
Like Maisie, from Accounts, pictured at her Amstrad,
smiling, who spent her holiday tramping the coast
to raise money for the inmates of one of *our* homes!
Fair Maisie—wait for it—slipped and broke a leg
while fording a flood! Some cretinous passing jogger
hitched her up and piggybacked her (ouch!)
to the nearest village. Now, back at her desk, she plans
to abseil down the face of Provincial Hall!
Really! I mean! ... If you can use your subversive skills
to disseminate this directive, photocopied
from a jotter, which outlines in barbaric grammar
procedures for privatising care of the gormless,
you will make an old man happy—and I might even
offer my grinning fizzog for rag number two.

7.

I pissed next to the Chief Executive today.
I am gratified that my grin quite staunched his jet.
He struggled to expel, wagged, and gave up.
A minor triumph for the natural aristocrats!
He growled something about the weather, as though
meteorology were the one thing he could not control.
I quoted Propertius to myself and answered nothing,
then appropriated the one washbasin graced with soap.
This must all sound petty, but one must grasp
the smallest victories in the face of the cosmic
humiliations to which one is daily subject. Talking of which,
here are details of the closure of your department
and guidance as to how to avoid standard recompense
in the face of union demands. If you should go,
please inform me a.s.p. of your successor.
I am so tickled by these wicked games!

8.

So. No quarter given. You stood and were counted
out; while I maintain the irony of an oblique
unfocused stance, like this dust-thronged angle of sun
bewildering the space I intend to inhabit
until I step into a pension. I know, now, that
is terrible: I watched the student spread his arms
and jig before the tank like a carnival cross;
and, as my friend lay dying (I've told no-one this)
loudspeaker vans traversed the city, exhorting us
to embrace change, as though we were not universes,
as though he were not a universe who filled his space
with elegance and tact; as though we were just function
not mystery; as though we could eradicate
our stories like a tape-machine. My whole schooling
was to survive. You can expect no more of me.
I shall remember you as someone I might have shared
some drinks with, but I suspect we have different
tastes and, although comrades in battle,
we might have found an evening a touch de trop.
Since I like my flat the way it is, and regular
Medoc, and visits to the sun, I hope my missives
remain unintercepted, and that your replacement
is trustworthy. Be all that as it may, I intend
to leak as frequently as someone prostate-plagued.
Please remember that, at your desk in the far province.

EXILED VOICES

The greatest violence done to people in our
society is to rob them of a public life.
           David Smail: *Taking Care*

1.

Scarred and thinned down this crackling line
you are finally a voice they could not make disappear.
It is as if I had stumbled on Villon's cell

the night before the promised gibbet:
a mouth close to earth, insistent on words.
But I see a hesitant host on New Year's Eve

bearing a fragrant curry and cool mint
and hoping to give pleasure.
I feel a rare loss with this click of your absence.

I feel a hopelessness for my species.
When that New Year struck
our clinking glasses made a true connection.

2.

It is Spring in this province.
I fill my attention with crocuses:
nests of gaping fledglings,
single-minded throats of zealots,

vaginal welcomings.
This garden hosts my last metaphors,
that act of colonising emptiness
for which I am losing taste.

I have a mistress with tresses
like a tree-shadowed waterfall
etcetera.
She is irrelevant in daylight

where I budget, under supervision,
the approved educational needs
of approved learners.
My body is provided for—

my teeth, my guts, my vision.
I am learning to use
the approved waste-bins
for my dreams: the melon-slice beaches,

the hot rocks above the sea,
the reeking night-clubs,
and the concerts with oriental soloists.
My transport is a twin-carburettor

overhead camshaft four-wheel drive
automatic coupé. I have
a casual user allowance
which I am learning to fiddle.

I have fantasised you
into someone who will understand.
The only reader
of the only thing I write.

Are you there?
I have received only silence from you
for so long. The reports
from your province

are approved and depressing.
I need your voice. I will understand
any code. If you do not write,
I will decipher that.

Two glistening blackbirds
are scuffling for space. They make
this lawn an emblematic
field of defiant

memory. Some ideas must be
ubiquitous as birds,
bright and pert as in
the distant regions of their coining.

3.

Every night, I am visited
by a ghost of buried tenderness:

in gusts and spasms
she delectably settles words on my tongue

in the deep lost hours of sleep,
vanishing as I rise to speak.

When I walk my fury like a dog
through Caesar's woodland

she catches my breath with the beginnings
of melting tunes that have no development.

Suddenly, in my magisterial green
chair, where I rigidly brood

on our ambushed naïve intent,
she insinuates into my muscles

a brimming forgiveness
soon spilt.

We chose the wrong weapons so carefully
from the Imperial Catalogue.

If I have a final journey
it will be mining inward

to lead her lovingly
into unreserved light

to be a spasm in Caesar's heart,
his fatal flaw.

4.

'The political context of our defeat':
I struggle to keep your words close to my heart

but they are like birds in autumn,
aimed elsewhere and swiftly vanishing.

They leave me in my familiar landscape:
a small boy in a drizzling fallout of guilt,

his hand in his pants or up a girl's
awaiting the chop.

We attempted the hero's world of arena and boardroom
but I never expected otherwise or more

than the happenings of this room:
a windswept desk and an empty phone.

It is a rehearsal for death
for which I have always been prepared

who barely managed to live, give or care.
And did I make Caesar tremble?

A few offered freedoms, a few hours
letting people talk, airing their battered dreams,

finding words that will not be marked out of ten.
We will not be allowed to use those words again.

I expected the juggernaut across my wrists.
I see you as Sisyphus, the world your stone,

shouldering upwards in history's spotlight.
But for me it was always darkness. I was always alone.

5.

They treat us like fools,
setting quite impossible tasks
and insouciantly turning away
to their rooms where the Silver Book
gleams like a blade.

What do they care about our dreams?
Little gracenotes and curlicues
around an iron tune.
They pay us, and life's
as simple as that.

Our room for manoeuvre
is twisting inside our own
contradictions.
Our energy flogs itself
with whips of strategy.

We are too clever by half.
Clauses, parentheses, footnotes,
ironic equivocations.
They went straight through the gates
to the heart of fear,

to the City-centre of self-love,
smiling from their tanks.
Look at our sisters, with their
garlands and blown kisses.
Look. There is your father.

A metal-barrelled pen
is tapping impatiently
upon your annual report.
Who wants to hear such things?
They belong to history and theory,

and warrant only qualifications
to cushion a name.
Spend a sabbatical on these things,
during which time the world
will have moved further

out of reach, into which
you will step blinking
and unaccustomed,
lucky to find your position
still open, narrowing fast.

6.

My passport said 'British'.
I resented that.
The boots slamming on continents.
The cuffs stiff with insensitivity
at the end of jungles.
I wanted to write 'English'
for its sly evasive music
and sensual valleys,
its twists and turns and unlocatable
laconic heart.
But that could not be tolerated.
They had to move me on
like a folk-song into a new setting,
atonal and without atmosphere.
'British' will do for that.

7.

If we had words like 'cell',
'interrogation', and 'been shot',

perhaps we might believe ourselves.
It's hard to live in a fuzzy watercolour

of dragged emphases.
What have we to complain about

except everything which is nothing?
We ought to get on with it

and think ourselves lucky.
If we speak for ourselves

that is poetry with a limited
circulation. If for others,

presumption. Silence has always been
quite good enough. It spawned us

and paid our way among bookshelves.
If we learned other languages

we should go there to speak them.
Life is handed to us on a plate.

It doesn't matter whose head it is.
Our punishment is that it is not ours.

8.

I have chastening news:
One year after slavery was abolished
in the old empire,
lost souls came wailing
to the hacienda
of their former master
begging for servitude.
They presented a book
with six hundred and twenty three reasons.

Perhaps it is time
to cultivate whatever gardens have been allowed us.

9.

Although our topic is pain, remarkably
it is like walking through a favourite garden
pointing out what is special about the flowers
and nodding. Let me tell you that your intent
to hurt by your angry flounce away will not
figure a damn or a jot. To those you would
wound, you have never been otherwise than some
varying indications in red and blue
columns. Your anger, that stain along your hair,
what your hands do at times like this, or how you
painfully yield up certain words—these things
have never counted, and this allows them to take
refuge in moods of quiet satisfaction
in heavily panelled rooms.
                         Our main concern
must be: How do we *stay*? There will be a moment
when they step off the edge of their agenda
and when the woman who is not expected to hear
has cleared their cups and listens. The sun will cook
the panels, and they will have to look somewhere:
at each other differently, or at the doodles
flowering at the edge of their minutes. That is
where I intend to inhabit, blood-boltered.
And are you to be there with me? Shall we try?

LETTER FROM ELSEWHERE

It was not quite as we'd imagined
when we honed the splendour of consciousness
housed in the bodies of the just:
I approached a sun-thronged lozenge

where woodland opened to a path
that tussocked down to a fordable river.
Water tickled my ankles. A few stones
slurred their green rondures. And I emerged

squelching through the pats of cows that were
technically barbarian into the daisies
and buttercups of an alien regime. I had crossed
the Border!

I felt all we'd prefigured
in those smoke-anguished rooms: I sensed
trained on my back the trembling
rifle-sights of death-starved guards.

I knew behind each copse the shaggy
welcoming figures waited with their
torturing altars and backlog of impotence
to be vented on my flesh. But—

the stream chattered gaily away,
cows munched and sputtered,
and if soldiers patrolled a barbed border
and barbarians cared, it was solely

in a collusive myth. So my stomp
through forbidden cowshit was brutally
deflating, warranting no publicity
of departure or arrival. If there are

checks to the foot, they are not located
in trip-wires or snipers, but in a kind
of love, a defining by relationship,
a need to be needed, as a hand

reaching for blackberries expects a thorn
to make an autumn ritual complete.
At last I stood as uneventfully
as hawthorn on the far bank, and the guard

who slammed lead punishingly through me
was Nostalgia: an intense sunlight
on abandoned hills; a song suddenly
perfected on a forgiven tongue. I live

in my chosen dream, have parted company
with the possibility of being elsewhere
but where daylight at this moment gleams.
I have no excuse for desire. And I envy you.

FATHER AND SON

*His reality became the form he achieved, the form
that does not lament transience or the vicissitudes
of history, but transmits an existence in peace.*
          Peter Handke: *Slow Homecoming*

My Father Begins to Tell his Story

A day arrives whose maples
shadow a room, their sway
distorting moons and waterfalls
that gazed their fictions from a wall

for years into a life. A magisterial chair
still fosters the unrenounced blue stare
that presided marriage, staunched its own
proclivities in children, and froze

itself in fury. But now the cheek
loosens with a wing of doubt. The eyes
curdle with the smoulderings of a tamped
story. What master is dethroned,

what rod snapped, to release this falter
of starved history from the locked dark?
Something approaches like a small conquest
while there is still time, while there remains

a father to confess, a son to hear,
softly merged by the enlacements
of Spring-haunted branches. One man
speaks for all when he revisits his silences.

My Father Reveals a Photograph

i

A sepia tent
mushrooms from leafwrack:

at once nostalgia
and a covert never quitted

where a boy crouches in vigil
at the taped flap.

He stares through a shaking
loss of focus,

his needs making their arrangements
stone-blind, butting at the light.

His palm extends
towards emptiness.

His mind is the ocean
on which it drifts.

ii

I stand in the valley of his gaze
where a fleet of headstones

drove at him under the moon
full tilt on their bone sea;

where a hunting owl
vanished like gunsmoke

and an apricot bruise
ripened into a sun.

Faded eyes
watch me that once

admitted the metaphors
of their own richness.

iii

He pitched his tent in the coal-hole
on his return, deep

in the webbed dust, stowing
the remains of trotters and bread

on the high shelf
where he had filched them.

He sallied, armoured and curt,
into the provenance of his dying

father, battening welds of unlikelihood
inside an album and a heart.

My Father's Last Meeting with his Father

It felt like a test failed:
his father slammed back

in the green chair, hawking
large nothings out of his lungs.

Above his head, the mantle
flared wings, a hummingbird

of exotic, irrelevant beauty.
He could not help this dying man.

When asked 'Where were you?'
he replied 'Nowhere'.

Later, he found a dusty
Klondyke nugget in the webbed

attic, and disappearing
windjammers on postcards.

No-one could tell him more.
Which was his inheritance.

My Father Sings in Church

On Sundays, a skinny Ulysses
coursed untrafficked ways,

fetching up on the granite islands
of city churches:

grimed hauteur, daunting
dank-holed cliff-faces, marbled

with bird-shit, to enter which
broached elaborate taboos,

troubling a deep lodgement
of unease.

Once, he risked
his voice against the holy

tact, unfurled
the Red Flag upward in a treble

dare. It returned
a tenfold

famished baying
through the stone forest.

My Father's First Job

He bore small walnut casks
fleetly across London

like Hermes, to customers
in high, chrome flats.

He hovered as they
swung lids on bronze hinges,

cupped ears like aviators
and fiddled crystal with fine probes.

When they smiled dreamily
it was all right, a tip,

and dismissal.
At last, his master beckoned him

to the bench, set
world-excluding horn over his ears,

and finger-and-thumbed a magic.
Glimpsed universes

trailed orchestras
and news. He travelled

henceforth like Tantalus,
excluded from a tasted

joy, tormented
by the unheard vastness of his gift.

My Father's Second Job

The gutters pig-pink.
Hands numb with lumped

innards. 4 am light.
Ultimate reduction

where women are dismembered
and no-one cares a fuck.

Iron-shod clogs
drag from ham to ham,

pig's skull to crimped tripes,
rippled brains to liver-slicks.

This mortuary
underpins Sundays,

river picnics, extravagant
leisured visions.

It breeds under nails, exudes
from pores. It guts

language of condition and purpose.
Its gaslight closeted you

in mountainous darkness,
flashed faces

of interred professionals.
Yet, one dawn,

braving the jeers,
she was there,

with film-star's legs
and jaunty pillbox hat:

your wife, my mother, who
led you to whisper

and touch, and the dared
instinct of redress.

My Father Talks of his Life and Death

All my life the presence of unlocatable
enemies; a whisper of malediction;
a ghostly hand guiding my life off-centre.

At my shoulder a timid god to placate;
in my bed a crooked conjuror of dreams
of fall whenever the day soared.

In the benevolence of my masters
a cage with a door swung open.
In their praise, the click of a lock.

My choice a rat's choice in a maze.
My prizes fringed with distant laughter.
My journeys predicted on secret maps.

I have emerged from their hands on this final
upwards slope. They can ignore
this unprofitable zero lunging at the air.

I remember you told me once of Villon,
wrestling for truth the night before the gibbet.
I have emerged into that, the cell whose keepers

no longer bother to observe. It is dark,
without whispers. I begin to walk
a long perspective which is purely mine.

A View from the Boundary:
for Stephen, soon to go abroad

An air of loss is streaming
at appalling speed
around this planet

rapt in this small
unmoving afternoon
Which is like being a father

who has not told his story
or invited yours
Which is more than red toys

raced on the carpet
and whittled miniature bats
for dead cricketers

on fag cards
or staring together
at terns on a windy coast

Which is more than poems
a creaking attic of poems
poised over your childhood

Now I have the boundary
and at my shoulder a profuse blackbird
and a view of lost skills

and a view of skills too late
acquired and the shock
of that swoop of yours

by which you announce yourself
This game accepts you
more than I ever did

I gave attention to nothing
but emblems
I froze the flame

for its meaning
A leaf casually falling
had to be perfected

by my grief
I never asked
Who are you

It was always
Where are you going
And now you are going

Soon you will not turn
when a bowler turns
but continue walking

across the outfield
over the boundary
quite out of sight

and into my mind
where I have always talked best
One November day

I saw on a hazel
white nuts in green
frills and tiny

clenched catkins both
there both
with a way to go

but both there
And I am both son and
father and that is

the flow we must
bite to the core
or taste nothing

which has been my taste
who have missed so many
boats in contemplating

perfect horizons
It is not enough
the opening of

sealed letters
for comfort
in estranged rooms

I have done that
It defines hell
A baffled part

of the whole story
of which this is
my stuttering start

like that bowler's
first steps whose run
will end in triumph

or temporary
redeemable setback
in a context

of adored imperfection
Above us as you play
a star of silver a plane

dwindles to nothing
as we do
silently while not seeming to move

Silently while not seeming to move
I have been approaching you
as my father unseen

for years arrived
one afternoon in my
authoritative green

armchair an old
upright man at last
stooping to admit

words to himself and me
'mistake' and 'dreamed'
and 'wish' and 'waste'

Man hands on misery
to man when he does
not hand himself

which means
I trust you
which means love

if anything does
And this is not to shoulder
and stagger with

another's confession
bidden to run
for him burdened

with his paraphernalia
when he could not
run himself

It is preparing
for complete death
leaving no ghost-

breeding scraps
no haunted
corridors in

the breathing house
It is to free
the steps of the living

from wading waters
of regret
We must re-invent

rituals for our
great concerns
starting with

holding one another
before journeys
taken alone

and learning to say
goodbye with proper
quittance

and if our only
myth is a quiet
game eccentrically

played where quirks
and lapses and luck
subsume themselves

to a small harmony
in a brief time
between an empty

field and an
empty field it is
no less a proper place

for needs to brood
upon themselves
and for a father

to begin to ask
forgiveness and say
Fare well

CHESS 1950

Pawn to King Four. All I knew.
Then Pawn to Queen Three.
Hunched opposite,
you taught me nothing

and beat me solid
game after game. Night after night.
Endless Slim Whitman
wailing a lost love,

endless finger-rolls
sweetening the air.
Poor sod, said my mother,
he doesn't know where she is.

Gambits, sacrifices,
your trembling hands
played them all.
Against me they won.

Opposite you
a new school tie
playing by the book.
The first page of the book.

Q.E.D.

When Taffy exhorted us
to give up bus-seats to women
'because there are often things happening to them
which we can't understand'

we looked at each other in wild surmise!
The more so as his eyes
swam in watery vagueness
and his chalk-stiff fingers throbbed the desk.

We wandered around quite stunned.
We thought of the high dark shelves in airing-cupboards
where mothers reached.
We hung at bus-stops and scanned the girls for clues.

He never told us more.
He resumed his fearful passion for thin lines
and equal-signs ranged one below the other.
Never again that throat-bunched tenderness,

that vision of unspeakable suffering
and the lyricism of male duty.
But the angles and curves of his geometry
were forever a muttered code at which we trembled.

HISTORY 'O' LEVEL

The French are all very well
when on the attack, but when their backs
are to the wall, they collapse.
Hence Alsace-Lorraine.

Disraeli was a Jew. His name
declares it. He was flashy
and suspect. Gladstone never did
those things with whores. He tried to save them.

There were no necrophiliac Pre-Raphaelites.
No pre-pube knocking-shops. The Boer War
was fought on unbelievably difficult
terrain. Rhodes (who was also a left arm

Yorkshireman who went in first and last
for England) was no spiv or thug
but an educator, a bearer of the torch
handed on to us by the Romans.

Those pink places are not scars
but where law is, and democracy.
And the copperplate that blazons this
grew from a Yorkshire Grammar School

where life was real, not like here
in the pulpy south. Next year think hard
before choosing against the discipline
of History, where you learn to discriminate.

HEADMASTER

'More Shelleyan gestures, Jones?'
Then a morning across the bells and breaks
wrestling with my wish to resign
a prefect's tasselled cap.

I was the angel of light,
he black with experience and compromise.
He sent me out once to buy a packet of Olivier.
I couldn't bring myself to offer one of mine.

On my side were Joyce, James Dean,
and a vague rive gauche:
white-faced black-haired women
and irrefutable epigrams.

He stood no chance.
At mid-day he admitted telephone calls,
rose, shook my hand, and said
'For my sake make one lyric that lasts.'

What did not last was his memory of me.
Twenty years later, that bristling
energy clamped into hieratic
chairbound splendour by a wrecked heart,

he gazed at me as into an empty sky.
Even my name was vapour vanishing.
He had too much future on his mind.
I saw then how he was forever

one of those faces at my shoulder
wincing or smiling at every word,
one of those I had to please or placate.
The ground control of every flight.

MY RIVER

All childhoods deserve a river
loitering through. Mine was brown Brent.
A field away and worlds away,
bending round and brushing flakey banks,

little spins upon itself like a brooding
man chuckling, and the green sleeked
hair of beautiful drowned girls.
Bald eyes of golfballs stared

from its unreachable shallows.
On Christmas Day it was an insouciant
cool stroller through the hothouse
bloat of groans and burnt tangerine-peel.

It understood my first love,
accompanying me like a Tchaikovsky clarinet.
Embedded in its deep grass
it taught me staring and the length of afternoons.

It churned or shivered like my spine
and was the slow feel of holidays.
It dreamed India for me with its kingfishers.
The secret untouchable soul grew under its willows.

Sleeplessness recalling it became a slow glide
towards invisible distances.
O it was all wellbeing, and stopped at an orchard
that sired small apples behind unbroachable wire.

NEAR GREENFORD, 1951

Like a vision it was unaccountable.
I parted branches and there it was,
totally absorbed with itself.
In old cream, with a fringed baldness,

the bowler six times looped a slow ball
like a deeply considered question,
and six times the batsman in his plum cap
leaned very attentively and returned an answer.

Six times. And time did not matter,
was utterly elsewhere.
There were fielders listening
and distant waiting batsmen in shadow

under trees listening. It was like staring
into deep water
at unexplained subtleties of light.
I was achingly excluded in another element.

Though I found my way back
it was never back to that:
perfect exposition, perfect refutation,
and something beyond them both, winning.

THE OFFER, THE REFUSAL

An inordinate Rolls de-created our street
to its cardboard and tarred lumps. It stopped
with a hint of shudder. This was the Boss.
He extruded a starched smile aimed at no-one.

Exiled to the kitchen, we craned at the hidden voices.
When he left, it was with embarrassed delicacy
as though someone should have tipped someone.
The car's velvet wake stirred a river of faces.

For the first and last time, my father gathered us
round. He said he'd been offered 'because I'm valued'
a loan to buy a real brick house. And had refused it.
We spent days stunned with grief and admiration.

Meanwhile, my father forked the passive earth
with vicious lacerating twists, brooding on how,
night after night, year after year, he had dreamed
his dismissal, after a prolonged trial for treachery.

AFTER TEMPEST

Il faut imaginer Sisyphe heureaux
          Camus: *Le Mythe de Sisyphe*

Four Poems Of Noëlle

1.

You found me among rubble
with the trace of a finger.
You separated
my enemies from my body
and shredded them with invective.

You tossed the Empire, all its
monuments and stratagems,
pomp and rigor, high in the air;
all my bitter envisaged redress,
my cold meal of revenge,

like a bomb of love. Furious against
the yearning creature's collusion
with its unnatural enemies,
the alignment with self-pity,
the pact with a wheedling past,

you doused the false lights
and scattered my fence of words.
'Don't curl like dead peel
over bitterness. Don't dance
to dead strings. Let's uncage eternity!'

2.

Born by the mythic sea
that witnesses and forgets
everything, except
what lingers in the air
when all the towers have fallen,

you are the inconsequent child
who compromises nothing, dancing
along the line of masks. You swat
the world's news like a cloud of gnats
and will listen only to the heart.

When I went missing, holing out
in ramshackle plywood under a neglected
orchard, that was where you were,
waiting to find me. 'Where else,' you smiled,
'Where else on earth was it possible to be?'

3. *A Moment from Algeria*

I conjure, here
by this whistling woodfire,
your schoolgirl's insouciant
pirouette into the Square

as volleys unbuckled
a soldier from his trappings
and his shocked eyes
caught as he fell

the echo of a lifetime's
yearning cry: you, in white
sprigged with lilac and rose,
flowering in a city

where ideal tortured ideal.
And you, what do you recall?
—'His eyes' bequest, the unaligned
unanswerable desire of creatures.'

4.

Tonight, there is a different noise:
speculative, like knuckles enquiring at a door
as if fearful it might be opened.
You are typing. You are gathering yourself

in those small trugs which are poems.
You are walking away down miraculous alleys
through that orchard where the fruit still hangs
to be picked and brought shining back.

You are making those marks like birdprints in snow,
like those faint lines on the grass of the camp
where people stayed, looked into our eyes,
and vanished like Troy. The noise quickens,

steps breaking into a run. I hear you leaving me
for encounters under trees, in a Church,
on a hot, distant shore. You are keeping
rendez-vous after all these years

with the waiting ghosts. Whatever you find,
embrace. They are what I mean
whenever I embrace you. I will be waiting, too,
to be found afresh, enlightened by your journey.

Walk by Storm-Wrecked Wood

White
as chicken-flesh
the scars.

The roots
broached
in walls of flint.

This the day
that chooses
to return

to me
the birds
of memory

from my lost
woodlands—
how they

sang
and in what
atmospheres.

Autumn

Last week
the house sang
with tempest,
and oaks

fell.
We studied
wreckage,
hearts broken.

Today
in windless
sunlight
leaves patter

and kiss
our hair
with manageable
deaths.

Nature

The thing itself
is silent.
Impatience battens

on the fern,
the mountain,
the tree.

And when
snow falls
it is

not enough.
And yellow
lilies

in a blue
vase
must bear

so much
of a particular
house,

and sunlight
touching them
is burdened.

At Stansted

The barn-roof
settles
in my gaze,

becomes
a curve
of my mind.

And I brought
here
so much,

so much
else
which now

is inches
of curve
of roof.

Snowstorm Viewed from Love

All shapes disband themselves
in this soft explosion:
the unfixed possibilities of the world
whirl and spin their primal courtesies

against the wall-eye of the universe,
deftly alone, untouching:
pure minimals of trees and homesteads;
clear notes of the resounding silence

at the heart of concertos, hectorings,
and consolations. Behind me
you sleep, whiteness
defining your shoulder,

your head received in whiteness,
and, beyond, the empty
whiteness smoothly awaiting
whatever colours I dream.

Tomorrow, I will invite you
to step into the aftermath
of turmoil, where sunlight
fires crystals across a huge

blank, into which our hands
will reach, to build
something like a man or woman
unflinching under a jaunty hat.

I Think of Sisyphus

endlessly resuming his endless task, thrusting
a rock upward on fate's down escalator,
as if, despite all the evidence, there smiles
Sense at the heart of things, that will one day plant

the rock on the summit, leaving only the question
To what end? Each inch—each grudged fraction
of inch—is achievement. Which is the only end.
And Sisyphus is blest, never condemned to stand

in his completed dream, the world applauding
or indifferent, cleaned of his investment
of sweat, the burden of a Nothing on a height
overlooking Nothing. He never knows failure—

the rock is always balanced against the future.
Sisyphus thinks he is asserting Hope. But he
is combatant with Despair. The despair of
gravity, and commonsense, and the laws of proportion.

He yearns as he shoves. On the desirable heights
the gods of limit preside. They cannot kill
Sisyphus, despite the tombstones of their vision.
His visionary eyes stare at his feet. He is

from **BURNING THROUGH THE FADE**

—an unpublished collection of poems
written since the publication of
Freeborn John (1990)

Acknowledgement is made where a poem
has previously appeared in a magazine

MANNEVILLE: THE MUSEUM OF RESISTANCE

It opens rarely, this museum.
It takes an emotional day
(liberation, important saints)
to spring it, like a unique flower
needing a certain slant of sun,
when the single door
will give into filtered light
beneath the cupola.
There is no charge to be scrutinised
by these faces that said *No*
or to stoop over maps starred for explosion
that describe, joltingly accurate,
the lanes I walk on Sundays
between hedges of thorn and beech.
A non-professional supervises
with a clear vocation elsewhere—
sheep, perhaps, or cider orchards.
It closes early to allow
a long quiet afternoon to spread itself
among creatures and people strolling.
The gaze of all this follows me
back down to the sharp nostalgia of *here*,
its choice between large and small coffees.

PN Review 129 (1999)

SEVERAL FLAUBERTS

To commemorate his savage
unanaesthetised dissection of us
we have severally erected
(a phrase he would have stored
with the slippers and the frillies)
his body (bloated with distaste)
and noble head (screamingly pressured
by our predictabilities);
first, against a quay
where boats slither fish
(as if the world
were endlessly spewing);
then, under a lamp
where moths collect
around assignations;
thirdly, in view
of a downtown café
and its reeking shadows.
Hammered by hopelessness,
bits of these hims
(who feared fathering a child)
begin to flake and fall
as he endures an eternal
re-enactment of his spawn—
a parked car shuddering its springs,
a man brushing a kiss away
as if moths bothered his lips,
and somewhere out of sight
(but obsessively seen)
the poisoned seep of stupid mouths.

Poetry Review Vol.89. No.4 (1999)

29 RIVERSIDE CLOSE HANWELL W7

Where there are so many absences,
barriers of space, perspectives
oddly aligned from dead windows,

there persists the struggle to stand
accurately where I once stood, with just
that way of looking, as if what was then seen

has no call to be otherwise: the tar-slimed
nuggets still to be loosened and kicked, the prefabs
a flotilla under the moon, Wendy just too fat

to be perfectly beautiful, but wholly loved.
I see me stumbling through this *somewhere*
naming it *bedroom*, or viewing blood-bruised currants

sprung from my father's lonely furious dig,
or her arms still pumping madness down
through suds. Time rids everything

but us of what we would keep, to become
this changed street we haunt and disbelieve,
this cul-de-sac where others are at home.

PN Review 137 (2001)

RENOIR'S GIRL

Years in moments, words
ripe as silence, glimpses
among trees or bruised walls

where, just hesitantly, and for
it seemed always, sunlight would not budge
and you not slip from it, and it

was for me to be there. And so
over and over again when I passed
from this—as a patch of light

caught and left that day the painted
patch of light on her shoulder, painted
to confirm how brief it was,

that dancing moment under the trees,
and how she turned to acknowledge who
perhaps was watching—I saw only

what was entering quiet reaches
beyond what I had framed, a forever
darkening towards not this.

PN Review 137 (2001)

AT MEOPHAM GREEN

The hawthorn curdles to its moment:
mayflowers swirled with dust
enter and quit perfection
seamlessly, their shadow
displacing edge after edge
of light. The season
turns like a gleam-bearing fish
slowly away into unresonant
darkness, and when we say
Dead, I shall leap all laws
to be with you, we feel
our bodies' upstream push against
time, as a woman wheels a child
into a pink avenue, to vanish
into a slumber of consciousness
where we would have all things
preserved. Voices of children
cram the air with chime
before a bell rings to clear
all play and leave a space, in which
we walk, sharing the weight
of something gleaming and precarious,
withdrawing, like colour from the flowers.

Navis 1 (1993)

DIFFERENT AND AGAIN

                This way I'm watching you,
across a peaceful lawn sprinkled
with blossom-fall, recalls those other
unspoken evenings, a tap-root
reaching back towards a myth
of deserving.
               Can you believe it?
These things to call ours? A hawthorn
lingering its cream into the dusk,
a telephone at rest and those we care for
moving silently beyond it,
safely undefined.
              We are not such fools,
of course. Or so we say. Or not say.
One day we will talk about this.
It will be an evening when only words will do,
colder, more circumspect, suspicious,
hand in hand and expelled,
              as when the box
was all but emptied and you lifted from it
two photos, stuck together by the years,
then parted them, as from a long kiss,
to find us, passion-gaunt and young,
burning through the fade.
             Remember now?
We do not learn, and that is our salvation.
A shutter blinks and we are there again,
gifted and unaware, just further towards
an outcome, whose form as this night falls
is grateful, hawthorn-drenched.

PN Review 129 (1999)

FROM THE ALBUM

        You sit distant, diminished,
beyond swags of lilac, where headstones
tilt in frozen urgency towards
a somewhere. I remember nothing of myself
although you crane in apprehension
towards what must be me.

        What must be me
stoops, focuses, and clicks you into
things passing, passed, to present you to whoever
will gather this from remnants we all leave
in an eventual room: not as we would have had it,
but, clearly, as it was.

PN Review 129 (1999)

TRAILS

The sky is so sensitive tonight, so skimmed
by the day's north wind, that five aircraft
raise weals of gold-pink upon it.
Some powder slowly into furrows,
then clouds, becoming finally a smear, a bruised smudge,
like resentment. Others, like a watercolour stroke,
drip a serrated fringe, then this too is withdrawn
into faint purple. In time the sky is like a back
long ago scourged, too long ago for anger,
perhaps even for the memory of its pain.
And then something is wiping it all away,
working at faint stains gently, spreading them
thinner but never quite removing,
until it is like old workings almost absorbed
into landscapes, as if nothing had ever yearned
to go anywhere, except inward,
and destination is absence, slightly troubled.

Previously unpublished

FORERUNNER

Widowed, she put up the barricades, these looping wires
around whose barbed rust the acacias
thickened their trunks, honeysuckle merrily prospered,
and holly welded its dark shine, slowly.
Where the hedge stayed stubbornly gapped
she hauled these half-doors, these crimped iron sheets,
until even the German soldiers hesitated
before a solitude so eerily sealed.
Now every day I'm the one who draws closer to her.
Planting a lilac, I find the worked black soil
of her potager, as the blade sinks smoothly
rooting ornament where she cropped necessity.
I see nut-trees slant their catkins like rain in sunlight
as fresh as when she saw them as a young wife.
I wonder if she heard in April these same three cuckoos,
or their forebears, including the one that coughs?
And these chaffinches, toppling their quick notes
into Pretty weird and Good to be here?
(What would she have heard in French?) Her gate,
a small wooden palisade, still chained,
stands next to our fleur de lys'd wrought entrance,
as natural now as old stumped hazel, hingeless,
screwed upright by bramble, and as I work at night
three iron rings where she hitched her cows to milk
hang buried behind plaster board, bookcase, books,
so far off, and barely a yard from my head.

Today, I saw the cherry tree she planted
flowering in splendour without her and, for a swirling moment,
without me. It was like turning a corner
and coming face to face.

Previously unpublished

RECOGNITION

Until today, when we saw a tail swayed like a wary cat's
on a forest post, and a dovegrey breast
barred like a hussar's, *cuckoo* had always been
bodiless, one of Spring's exuberant throwaways,
pure chime rebounding from sappy timbers.
But here it was, a particular, awkward bird
balancing its weight till the effort wasn't worth it
then launching off into a hard swift flight,
so that *cuckoo*, in however many Springs remain,
will always be that bird on that post, that flight,
just as, as you watched it, that smile of yours
poured down from a hillside eighteen years before
when you turned in a white dress sprigged with orange flowers
to gaze in delight through a gather of marguerites
not at a bird but at me, suddenly stopped, incredulous
to be so recognised, hardly daring
(is this me?) to climb nearer.

Previously unpublished

OCTOBER

It's autumn, and suddenly great weights of life:
a cricket like a wheat-ear ready to burst,
flaking, one crooked rear leg missing
so that levering upwards on the doorpost
it curves and falls and starts again and pauses
to feed with fastidious foreclaw its ascetic head
or to nibble a claw clean, elbows out—
so human, I shudder—its raggedness, its loss,
its pointless scraping across earth to start again and again;
and butterflies in opulence,
peacocks, red admirals, golden-winged field-browns
spanning wasp-eviscerated pears
to sweeten their velours with long probes,
their slightly tattered wings flattened
to solar panels against the ground, some on the roof
scanning the slates for heat with wings down-tipped;
and heavy birds quite public, the woodpecker,
its symmetries of green and black
shuddering to the red drill of its skull,
and a pair of jays glamorising mist-hung brambles,
lobbing grenades
of screeching colours as they hop and soar
back to the woods, where a death-touched patch of leaves,
a yellow outrider among lingering greens,
strikes a tree with a hot light worthy of July.

PN Review 137 (2001)

CHEZ

In April, they bring the gnomes down from the loft,
red-hatted, blue-eyed, from their hibernation
and distribute them across the lawn,
spaced evenly, in little groups of consolation.

Their dog throws himself again and again
against the chain's maddening short range
as we approach across the trim white gravel.
We smile, he yaps, in the usual exchange.

They set four bottles for aperitif
in a surround of dishes piled with gold
and tawny flakes and chunks, then stand
awkward and smiling, as if their house is sold

and we have bought it. Soon their daughter,
shy, grinning, with her year-old son appears
from the smaller house across the lane
the whole family have spent two years

rebuilding from a few stones up.
And then their son, also across the lane,
from the larger criss-cross timbered house
his granny died five years ago in, *In pain*

but drugged, praise be to God.
A silence is served first, that gap
torn raggedly against the grain by death.
Then monsieur remembers and fills the glasses up.

They talk gran slowly with us until we see her
sitting right there. Then the talk moves on.
Time now for a tour around this house
from which the dead and children are never gone.

Timbers we've featured they've plastered over.
Talking heat systems they show us round with pride.
They've raised the ceilings that we bang our heads on.
On different journeys, for a while we coincide

and, like the passengers on trains that pass each other,
are left with strange longings. Monsieur
comments on my study, all those books,
and Madame warns They'll help to pass the winter.

Back past the dog still hoping to break the chain.
The daughter's meadow-land's awash with sun
that juts a shadow from each garden feature.
No gnomes. But owls, bears, toads. All spaced alone.

Previously unpublished

OSCAR THE DONKEY

Whenever I leave, he points his muzzle
skyward, and wheezes desolation,
until from that wheeze are pumped
air-thumps of such tragic pressure

I always turn back (saying *just once*)
to offer daisy-starred rips of grass:
a man and an animal engaging awkwardly again
across more than wire.

Because I do not understand,
because I have no notion of his notion of my words,
and know only what I know of grief,
I envisage in that staring head

vast imprisoned needs occasioned by love
which I must halt for,
the way I let my cat
appropriate the sacred, anxious space

between my pen and the waiting page,
let her sit there, purring,
because she is old (does she know that?)
and adores me (is this true?)

If I walk on a little way,
he will dip his head and amble after.
I fear the farmer—no sentimentalist—
might huffily pasture him elsewhere

or that I will one day return
to find him absolutely gone.
And so I do walk on a little way
to store in memory that muffled stumble

parallel with my walking, a little behind,
one of those treasured coherences
remaindered among things gone away
or going, a small narrative

whose conjunctions are what love imagines.
Tonight, I use my words to brim
every hoof-dent with moonlight,
float dew on every neck-hair caught on the wire.

Previously unpublished

A BIRTH

The cow peers behind her, then away
back into the sky where she had thrown her voice
and for a moment the calf
cling-filmed like a gift
shines in the great indifference
of its own and sudden being
until the cow turns, lumbers up, claims it
with pushing snout and lariat tongue,
and the calf squirms, unfolding limbs,
at this injunction to be more than be.

Previously unpublished

NIGHT OF SEPARATIONS

Tonight the cows are crying out under the wind.
Several men, stamping through mud, have removed the calves
leaving the field to cows and to their anguish.
(I find this a difficult word).
So the calves are orphaned and the cows unchilded.
(These are also difficult words).
Perhaps the wind will close it all down
and in the knife-edged dawn there will be no (grief)
and no sign of the lost (infants).
Hot milk will pump into weeping casks
that have no lips and cannot grow.
But at this moment, this moment under the wind,
(anguish cries into absence and it feels forever).

Previously unpublished

DAY OUT

What should be (as I imagine it is
for these bodies lounging in the salt-edged sun)
a partial switch-off from time, becomes,
as the foam-laved sand shifts beneath my feet
like time itself, an urgent recall
to the small room of poetry-making
where, like a goblin from some northern tale,
I must sweat against time to make something
starlike, sharp and hard,
to hang like light struck from the flint of forever
above the drift of what we do with days.

Previously unpublished

FROM VOLTAIRE'S GARDEN
AND OTHER ENTANGLEMENTS

'Je sais seulement que la terre tremble depuis deux ans et que les hommes ensanglantent la surface depuis longtemps. Que faire a tout cela? Cultiver son jardin et sa vigne.'
                    Voltaire: *Letters*

1

It's instructive, being stared at by stones,
their cool, Socratic way of asking '*And?*'
so that no thought is ever final, even adequate.
Severely unlike those compliant faces
of yesteryear (O neiges d'antan!) their beaming
encouragement of my brainy glissandoes!
Nothing congratulates or rewards, you see.
I recently looked up from those pitiless stones
to find cows, in line, just gazing at me.
The scanning animal scanned, imagine it!
In those remorselessly receiving eyes
I was simply a small accident of presence
that would disappear when they chose to turn away,
a *something* that was about to have had its moment.

2

When my neighbour (he lives a mile away)
stopped at the gate to *chat* (so much to learn!)
and asked whether I did not feel nostalgic
for my *homeland*, I replied
'I do, yes, but no more than when I lived there.'
(For a moment, I felt quite like my old self!)

3

It's tempting, after a bruising,
to prefer the company of beasts.
They have the beauty of limit.
My cat's appeal
is commensurate with its being entirely cat
and stalking back into cat darkness
at outlandish offers of extension
(spiced and garlicked sausage, for example).
But I thought I'd found stupidity even here,
among the creatures. Two mated great-tits
built their nest inside the bulbous top
of a black and cast-iron cream-maker I'd heaved
from its stog in brambles and re-positioned
by the gate-post. As the sun beat down,
this assumed the furious qualities of an oven.
I imagined a slow roast of chicks, and strapped
an umbrella to the gate-post, for the shade.
I then realised (like a savage) *the sun moved!*
and every hour I realigned the spread
to keep the shadow slap upon the nest.
Nine days I gave to this, peering in
from time to time to check the throats were gaping.
On the tenth day, one by one, the chicks
spilled out and were eaten by the cat. (Again,
existence tightrope-walking the twin plunges
of farce and tragedy!) For a while,
though grieved by those brief-fledged futilities,
I hugged the little comfort of my deed—
a good act is a good act is a good act—
but then (O those gazing stones!) the slip and slur!
No thought is ever final, even adequate.
Whose flesh was roasting in that furnace? *Mine!*
Perhaps great-tits not philosophers know

what's good for great-tits. (So much still to learn!
And all so obvious!) Perhaps imagination,
empathy—those humane virtues—had disturbed
the rhythms of great-tittery, leaving chicks
to sway dizzily unprepared, before their time,
on their launching pad above a patient cat.

It's tempting, after a bruising,
to prefer the company of earth.
For two days after, I *tilled the soil*
for its black, rich-scented peace.
                      And the blank stones
rose in stare.

4

Deciding whether or not to remove brambles
(in my case, fifty yards of them, eight yards deep)
is an involved and thorny matter.
To start with, it's perfectly possible to live with brambles
(and my instinct, after all, has always been
that all change is for the worse).
And then do I want to lose the morning glimpse
of rabbits bounding in and out the tangle?
Or autumn's sensual gift
of berries on the lips and tongue?
(You see, I'm using the present tense,
the relaxed shrug of hypothesis,
as if I'm toying with possibilities.)
In reality, I birthed the future barbarously.
I hired a machine and in two days ripped them up,
leaf, stem and root. I piled them high,
house-high, to dry for an autumn burning.
As I drove, I feared my passage,
would be one of squash and mangle—gobbets
of ears, paws, skulls and tails—but I swear

I touched no creature (at least no furry one).
They'd all decamped, with visionary wisdom.
There's a scatter of trees there now,
(I planted them too close, but let that be
a problem for inheritors),
native trees, hazel, hornbeam and beech,
and, as summer progresses, astonishing stands
of foxglove, stately, brooding, ominous
(the way I like things).
There are clumps of ox-eye daisy, too,
and spindly plants that flaunt, in the slightest breeze,
their pinpoint yellow flowers.
I call these *nipplewort*, from my wildflower book.
(Although I've never confidently identified
so much as the simplest flower from its pages,
the magnificence of that word, *nipplewort*—
its mincing, sexy start
and resonant, vulgar finish—pleasures me
more than Linnaean accuracy).
I know! I know! I can hear you muttering
Shilly-shallying! Everything but why!
O, but that *why* was painful,
the answer to it staring back at me
pitilessly from the stones—
what fuelled me behind that gross machine
to a slavering frenzy of deracination
was no dream of wildflowers gulping light and air
but a gut-fear of invasion,
of spiked intricacies on the rampage
stalking my land like the rim of an eclipse,
remorseless, cosmic—eight yards, then ten, then twelve.
Space closing down. Light dying.
(You see me here, who never risked a metaphor,
embracing the farthest meanings of nearest things!)
It was the way my furious relish
outstripped me that left me trembling by the heap
of writhing stems and weeping roots,

the way my reasonable hands could lavish slaughter
like the last act of some demented gardener!
(And do you know I fear to swim as well,
to feel my feet
lift from the sand and hover over
I know-not-what unnamed uncategorised beast?
I never admitted this, the days I lay
at the sea's edge, conspicuously clever,
drafting *Candide*).

5

My land hosts two ancient trees.

The one exudes small teardrop pears
that ripen yellow, then bronze,
softening only
some days before their fall.
Through dark spatters, like finger-bruises,
glitters surface
to scab like tiny salt-pans,
but sweet,
hosting green-gold gluts of flies
that when wasps muscle in
scare violently, like a bottle shattering.
As if freighted with a dust of this sweetness
the surrounds of air pasture tiny creatures
that jig on the elastics of their needs.
So all day this tree seethes
behind its palisade of suckers
as if furious with itself and with the world.

Death has bleached the other
and sun and wind scour it.
There's just an essential trunk
and the stumps of what had been branches.

On these, butterflies spreadeagle themselves
and throb symmetrically in demure
ecstasy against bone-hard silver.
Nothing else happens. Just those
great-eyed wings
staring at the sun
and the sense of crash
come autumn, come the winds.
They stand a few yards apart,
themselves, and oddly right.
And now *I* arrive—an unbidden
restless third
trying like mad to describe things *as they are*.

6

Some days, I find it hard to keep
my lips kinked in my trade-mark goat-smile,
(that taut little dip, remember? that tightrope-walk
above stupidity, pain and pointlessness?)
Today, for instance, a day that started
with a vile wind smuggling sand-grains under my skin,
and snapping an apple-tree in the distant field,
brought me first, unasked, news of the idiot world
(it's my passing neighbour, who's chosen to convert
our *chat* into a daily bulletin) where ten thousand troops
are being mobilised (no change there then)
for the next war (nor there) and the rising sea,
drawn ever upwards by the magnet
not of the moon but our *special* (from *species*)
ineptitude, has swept away whole towns (built on the sites
of other towns previously swept away).
Despite which, my grimace might have survived
had it not been for the bull in that same far field:
I watched him endlessly ambling up to cows
to sniff, and being endlessly disappointed,
consoling himself

with a quick scratch against the shattered tree.
Ahead of him lie three years of this, just this:
frustrated hopes, with the occasional *Zowee!*
then they'll cart him off for slaughter. It got to me,
I do admit, in my vulnerably lowered state
it really got to me! I saw us blundering around
like a lust-crazed bull, enjoying our few
spasms on a string of nothing,
unconjoined self-pleasuring moments,
witticism, orgasm, metaphor. And then—
the knacker's yard!
Behold me then—
Enlightenment Scans the Abyss of Despair!
except I did not feel
generic, merely a huddled one-off, hugging
my infinitely meaningful body
against *unthinkable* void!
Irrational, I know! As for that smile—
when I saw the bull sniff pointlessly once more
and bash its doleful head against the tree,
I did feel my lips flicker—but then settle
into a shape of pity, grudgingly.

7

This man has entered my life. Not his words
(we scarcely understand each other)
but the gravid bulk of him, his gentle shouldering
of so much I'd thought valuable to the sidelines.
Awaiting him, I struggled at my hedge
with a druidical curved saw and skewed ladder,
and was mutilating hornbeam when he arrived.
He drove an orange tractor that puttered fruitily
behind which a trailer bounced, like an emblem
of puppyish anticipation. The tailboard down revealed
a family of coffins! His, Hers and Theirs,
in jointed oak that would make it through to Judgment!

But they held no death. Each one (his handiwork)
was compartmentalised with plywood walls.
In the first, a chainsaw neatly filled the length,
accompanied (each in its section) by a chain,
a key, a flask of fuel, screwdriver, spanners,
a stiff-bristled brush, a foursquare folded duster,
and a little conical brass container
for clicking machine-oil.
The second was lined with blades, straight, curved and stumped,
hafted with ash, the smaller sections filled
with a range of files, an oiled rag, secateurs,
and a small carborundum wheel
fitted with flex and plug.
The third held his accoutrements: an orange helmet
with visor and ear-pieces, two pairs of gauntlets
(one specially toughened for brambles and acacia)
a one-piece lightweight waterproof, sunglasses
and three packs of paper handkerchiefs. In the fourth
(so small, mysterious!) odd, disconcerting objects
adrift from a clear purpose: peg-like prongs
looped with small chains and topped with iron rings,
a short-handled spade with cut-off scimitar blade,
a clutch of little plastic flags, triangular,
jutting from six-inch stems. *This was his mole-box!*
He'd noticed an incipient plague
and come prepared!
('But only' he said, sensitive to my shudder,
'if you want me to.')
Also in the trailer, lying loose,
a pine rod, an exact two metres long,
(to cut the hedge to a consistent height)
and metal poles, planks and two small wheels
which became a movable scaffold. Last of all,
at the back of the trailer, an old car-tyre
and a plastic bottle engorged with sump-oil.
By twilight, the hedge was cut, the lopped waste
trimmed into logs (stacked by the shed), the twigs
and rotten branches slung into the trailer,

driven down the lane to a field (he'd fixed this
with a farmer-friend), tipped out and burned
(the fire started with the oil-rinsed tyre).
A whisky-aperitif (after, of course, a meticulous
stacking of boxes and trailer) and he'd gone.

I lay wide-eyed and thought-racked. A sleepless night.
I needed to *place* him, find the *essence* of him,
and all I could see was *difference*. There am I,
forever opening my mouth, dipping my pen,
gushing words like a frog its spawn,
with every phrase a winch of superiority
cranking me further adrift from the world,
while he *lies in close*, says little,
endlessly adjusts (so detailed!) his every act
to the grain and character of things. At last
I did doze, only to start bolt upright
with the truth of it resounding in my ears:
Everything is more important than him!

The following night
as I drove up into the darkness of his village
to pay him, trees, signposts, homesteads
flashed out fresh-made to greet my headlights
and I doodled at philosophy again
spurred by these poignant presences scattered
through a great murk, under distant stars!
When I reached his house, I crunched the gravel path
up to the glazed door. And there I stopped.
My hand was raised to knock, but could not knock.
He sat in a high-backed chair. There was a girl
(I've no idea her age, I remain
hopeless with children) his grandchild, I think,
perched on his knees. She was playing with cards
spread on the long oak table. He was smiling
and leaning back. It was the space that shocked me,
the silent space between them. It said

I do not matter. I am here for her.
I am what she will leave behind and sometimes remember.
And he was wholly that. It was enough.
There was no book, glass of whisky, TV screen,
radio music, gardening journal. His hands
lay still and empty upon the chair's arms.
He was where I have never been, *just there!*
I stood, wholly excluded from what I saw,
then backed off, after jamming the money
(sadly, the one thing that connected us)
under the door. I drove back home
past the same scattered homesteads, signposts, trees.
And my cleverness had nothing to say about them.

8

I find I've started to make small gifts, *bequests*,
the way some matrons suddenly unload
on daughters and grandchildren necklaces,
ear-rings, entissued lacy gloves
worn once, that evening…
so that it seems a familial distribution
of pretty things she'll never use again
until some thick-skinned know-all blows the gaff:
Mother! How morbid! You're good for ages yet!

It began—things do—with an unrelated act.
Cleaning the land, I stumbled (literally!)
on detritus of other lives, people who'd moved
in similarly clogged boots across this earth
to make their mark, leaving flowers, bushes, paths,
elaborate beds or bridled wilderness,
epigraphs of their taste (all withered, overgrown,
submerged, or formless). Ironically (of course)
what had kept some shape and sent me sprawling,
or snagged my fork and rake, were rusted
inadvertent scatterings—blades, barrel-hoops,

chain-links, locks, prongs—broken, abandoned things.
The *unprized*, which, *ipso facto*, had survived!
I hung these from the trunk of a dead tree
to make an *open-air museum*. They creaked and flaked
through season after season. Atop them all
I placed the remnants of a mask or helmet
found tangled in a rambling shrub, (a *helmask!*)
vague enough with rot to have performed
in any of three wars. (Its sockets track me,
and, when I'm close to it, my flesh responds,
as if everything is still and always happening.)
But I digress (I think). One morning, stooping
at yet another toe-stub, my fingers closed
not on the latest trove to hang or dangle
but on something a few weeks earlier they'd let drop—
a pair of secateurs, the curved blades plunged
in earth—a kamikaze parakeet!
And then I found my hand-fork, one prong snapped,
discarded, and discovered now where ivy
was already fingering up and claiming it
like the past made visible. What was *less* visible
was me! I felt the air beginning to slip
through and past me! I was becoming one
with the *disappeared*, whose only traces
are cryptic debris on a dead tree-trunk!
So the seasons will recur like stillness
while I slide across them into absence,
strewing strange elliptical mysteries
that pose the question *Who?*—unlike the shrill
I'm here! of the hand-span of my tomes.
There's a charm in this, a kind of puckish wit
(a goat-smile coming on?) so I'm lending
chance a hand. I've *chained* that misplaced brolly
(the one, remember, that parasolled the chicks?)
to the stone gate-post. In time new generations
of passing neighbours or proprietors
will halt amused, imagining

from that wind-chewed posturing skeleton
a creature that might once have strained for flight
and never made it, or a clawing hand
that vainly tried to write words on the wind!
So, this grinning rationalist will have vanished into
metaphor! How I *like* that! (I've often pondered
on the right wrong-footing way to leave the stage!)

PN Review 201 (2011)